WHAT WOULD YOU DO IF....?

What Would You Do If... ?

*Fun and Creative Ways
to Teach Your Kids Spiritual Values*

Greg Johnson

Servant Publications
Ann Arbor, Michigan

Vine Books is an imprint of Servant Publications especially
designed to serve evangelical Christians.

All Scripture references, unless otherwise noted, are taken from the
Holy Bible, New International Version. © 1973, 1978, 1984
International Bible Society. Used by permission of Zondervan
Bible Publishers. Selected references have been taken from the
Living Bible (LB), © 1971 by Tyndale House Publishers. All rights
reserved.

Published by Servant Publications
P.O. Box 8617
Ann Arbor, Michigan 48107

Cover illustration by Warren Dayton, Prints of Peace
Cover design by Diane Bareis

95 96 97 98 99 10 9 8 7 6 5 4 3 2 1

Printed in the United States of America
ISBN 0-89283-855-8

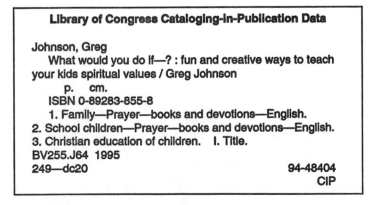

Library of Congress Cataloging-in-Publication Data

Johnson, Greg
    What would you do if—? : fun and creative ways to teach
your kids spiritual values / Greg Johnson
        p.   cm.
    ISBN 0-89283-855-8
    1. Family—Prayer—books and devotions—English.
2. School children—Prayer—books and devotions—English.
3. Christian education of children.   I. Title.
BV255.J64 1995
249—dc20   94-48404
                                                         CIP

Dedication

To all the moms and dads who want to lead spiritually, but don't know how. I hope this book starts many great discussions about things that are eternal.

Contents

Read This First / 13

1. The New Kid on the Block
(accepting a handicapped child)** / 17
2. Buried Treasure (honesty with money)** / 18
3. Phone Phrustrations (lying)* / 19
4. The Family That Forgot to Say It (saying "I love you")** / 21
5. Sticks and Stones... (handling insults)** / 22
6. The Eyes Have It (cheating)** / 24
7. Who, Me? (serving)** / 25
8. When the Doorbell Rings (responding to tragedy)* / 27
9. Is a Half-Truth Better than No Truth?
(telling the whole truth)** / 29
10. The Shopping Mall Caper (doing what's right)** / 31
11. A NOTEworthy Difference (envy)** / 33
12. The Herd Gives the Word (peer pressure)** / 35
13. The Listening Type? (taking advice from parents)* / 37
14. The Accident (respecting someone else's property)** / 38
15. Close Friends? (loyalty)** / 40
16. Bored to Tears! (boring Sunday school)** / 42
17. Thrifty, Cheap Or... (selfishness)** / 44
18. More Excuses than Time (Bible reading)* / 46
19. Pair Pressure (pressure to pair up)** / 47
20. How Good Is Your Word? (keeping your word)** / 49
21. How to Knock Shock Jocks (discernment)** / 51

* CHAPTER FOR CHILD(REN) TO READ ALOUD TO PARENT(S)
** CHAPTER FOR PARENT(S) TO READ ALOUD TO CHILD(REN)

22. Avoiding the Root of All... (loving money)** / 53

23. Watch Your Yap (choosing your words)* / 54

24. The Winning Edge (pride)** / 56

25. Some Things Just Aren't Funny
(inappropriate jokes)** / 58

26. The Kid with No Boundaries (what's best for you)** / 60

27. Tuning In to the Right God
(responding to the right God)** / 62

28. The Mouth That Wouldn't Stop (gossip)* / 63

29. She Changed the Rules (responding to unfairness)** / 65

30. The Empty Chair (compassion)** / 67

31. Back Row High Jinx (respect for church)** / 69

32. Some Things Are Immovable (responsibility)** / 70

33. How Much Is Enough? (contentment)* / 72

34. My Friend... the Spray Painter (real friendship)** / 74

35. Trying to Measure Up (envying a popular kid)** / 76

36. How to Get Clean (guilt)** / 78

37. "Umm, Excuse Me... (disagreeing with authorities)** / 80

38. The Unexpected Question (boldness)* / 82

39. Nice Interception (giving another a break)** / 84

40. Remembering You Have It All (thankfulness)** / 86

41. The Overnighter (pitching in)** / 88

42. Whom Will You Choose to Win? (unselfishness)** / 90

43. Layoff (handling major disappointment)* / 92

44. On-Line Answers (homework)** / 93

45. Rubbing It In (sportsmanship)** / 95

> * CHAPTER FOR CHILD(REN) TO READ ALOUD TO PARENT(S)
> ** CHAPTER FOR PARENT(S) TO READ ALOUD TO CHILD(REN)

46. Taking the Fall for a Dirty Dog (taking responsibility)** / 97

47. Turning the Other... (fighting)** / 99

48. The Fifteen Dollar Dilemma (honesty)* / 101

49. Caught with Your Mouth Open
(tough situations)** / 103

50. Getting Even (the Golden Rule)** / 105

51. The Church Camp Dilemma (integrity)** / 106

52. Pennies from Heaven (using money wisely)** / 108

53. Two Ticked-Off Drivers (anger)* / 109

54. To the Rescue (sticking up for the defenseless)** / 111

55. Dad's Big Helper (helping out)** / 112

56. Packaged Treasures (sharing)** / 114

57. The Vicious Loudmouth (seeking revenge)** / 116

58. The Skeptical Neighbor (going easy on doubters)* / 117

59. Christmas Expectations
(rejoicing with those who rejoice)** / 119

60. The Basketball Nightmare (humility)** / 121

61. "I Can Take Care of Him, I Promise"
(responsibility with animals)** / 123

62. Answering Tough Questions (describing God)** / 124

63. "Here Am I, Send... (motives)* / 126

64. Choose Wisely (choosing friends)** / 127

65. Light-Fingered Friends (stealing)** / 129

66. Speaking Up Is Hard to Do
(persecution as a Christian)** / 131

67. The Chatterbox (responding to discipline)** / 133

---

* CHAPTER FOR CHILD(REN) TO READ ALOUD TO PARENT(S)
** CHAPTER FOR PARENT(S) TO READ ALOUD TO CHILD(REN)

68. The Big Letdown (giving encouragement)* / 135

69. The Tough Guy (gloating)** / 136

70. The Fruit of Your Labors (bragging)** / 138

71. What a Chore! (chores)** / 140

72. The Captain's Tough Choice (love)** / 141

73. Leave It Where You Put It (prayer)* / 143

74. He Still Does Miracles (responding when God answers prayer)** / 144

75. The "One Up" Game (the right type of humor)** / 146

76. Where Freedom Can Lead (too much of a good thing)** / 147

77. When Believing Isn't Seeing (faith)** / 149

78. 'The Least of These... (generosity)* / 151

79. Rebuffed? (being hasty)** / 152

80. Friday Night Fights (saying "I'm sorry)** / 154

81. Taking the After-School Challenge (smoking/drugs)** / 155

82. Only One Way? (salvation)** / 158

83. The Whole Truth and Nothing But... (parental integrity)* / 160

84. How Much Does Friendliness Cost? (loving the unlovely)** / 161

85. What to Do when You're Ready for More (being faithful in small things)** / 163

86. It's Not if You Win or Lose, It's... (fairness)** / 165

87. It Doesn't Get Much Worse than This (your worth to God)** / 167

---

* CHAPTER FOR CHILD(REN) TO READ ALOUD TO PARENT(S)
** CHAPTER FOR PARENT(S) TO READ ALOUD TO CHILD(REN)

88. Promises, Promises (keeping your word)* / 169

89. Unhappy Camper (complaining)** / 170

90. Early Riser (spending time with God)** / 172

91. Follow the Leader? (peer pressure)** / 174

92. To Go for the Goal, You've Got to Pay the Toll
   (laziness)** / 175

93. Charting His Own Course–Sort Of (patience)* / 177

94. The Unpardonable Sin? (forgiveness)** / 179

95. The Confused Sub (respect for adults)** / 180

96. Look Out for the Power of Evil! (Satan)** / 182

97. What's Worthless? (discerning good from evil)** / 184

98. The Costly Deception (parental forgiveness)* / 186

99. What Are You Known For?
   (having a good reputation)** / 188

100. No Comment for Everything (not being thanked)** / 189

101. Inside Choices (true happiness)** / 191

* CHAPTER FOR CHILD(REN) TO READ ALOUD TO PARENT(S)
** CHAPTER FOR PARENT(S) TO READ ALOUD TO CHILD(REN)

Read This First

We all know that time is a nonrenewable resource. Once it's gone, we can't retrieve it. The older I get, the more I wish this weren't the case. Though it seemed like forever before both of my boys were out of diapers, now that they're approaching their teenage years, time is whizzing by! The reason? Like most, we're a busy family.

Amid this busyness, I have a confession to make. I'm not very good at getting everyone together for family devotions. I've tried to blame it on our hectic schedule, and the fact that a family time around the Bible or a formal discussion of Christian values was never modeled for me. But even with these built-in excuses, I still feel like I should be doing something.

For some reason, no family devotional books or Bibles have ever caught my eye. *What I need*, I thought, *is something quick I can do during the dinner hour a few nights a week that will get us talking.* So I wrote these 101 "what if" situations.

Today, if I can get my sons to the table early, we'll have devotions so Mom can listen in while she gets the meal ready. (I do breakfasts, not dinners!) Sometimes, since I'm usually the first to finish eating, I'll read a chapter while everyone else is taking their last bites. I've even used these short readings in the morning before school or later in the evening around bedtime. We usually read about three or four a week.

What I'm doing–and intend to continue doing–is redeeming the time. I'm fairly good at spotting teachable moments, and I'm a pretty consistent model. But doing something intentionally spiritual, especially while our kids are in grade school, is difficult, though *very* important. This book has been a good tool. It allows my children to use their imaginations. As you go through this with your family, help your children use theirs.

This book will work best if you adjust the names and genders as you read. That way you'll be able to personalize this book for your family.

- Do you have all boys (like me)? Then alter the story while you read it so it fits them.
- Do you have all girls? Then do the same.
- Do you have one or more of each? Well, then you have your choice: target the situation to whomever it best applies, or add the necessary pronouns so you're reading for both boys and girls.
- Do you have older kids who will be at the table? Then include them when it's time to debrief the situation. Use their words and experience to help teach your grade schooler.
- If you have younger children, allow the words spoken to soak into their young minds. After the lesson, let them ask questions if they still don't follow what's going on.

Remember, the goal is to read each "what if" situation in such a way that grade schoolers really believe it's about them. Honest responses are the key, so their answers should never be judged or criticized. Let the questions help them to think and the Scripture passages to make the point. Above all, avoid "preaching." The grade school years are a good time to convince your children you can *listen to* and *accept* what they say. (This skill will *definitely* come in handy later on.)

About every fifth reading, it will be YOUR turn to answer the "what if" situation. If one doesn't exactly apply, don't let that stop you from using *your* imagination. Oh yes, *let your grade schoolers read the "what if" situation to you.* They'll have fun, it'll break up the routine and it will give you a great chance to model honesty for them!

The Questions

I've tried to keep them simple, but each child is different. If your child can't clue-in to the question, rephrase it or go on to the next. Remember, the goal isn't just to get the right answer, it's to get an *honest* answer.

Those Bible Passages

As you'll notice, each lesson finishes with two or three Bible verses that relate to the "what if" situation. I have deliberately left off any questions to add to the discussion. Does that mean you shouldn't ask any? No, not at all. If you have extra time and can ask questions about the verses that your children can answer, go ahead, dig a little deeper.

One last thing: find a book mark to use so you don't lose your place. Have fun!

1 ■ The New Kid On the Block

What If...

Three doors down from our house a new family moves in. As they unload the big yellow Ryder truck, you see them haul a swing set into their backyard and a boy's bike into the garage. *What does that mean?*

That's right, they have a kid—probably one your age.

Though you already have neighborhood friends to play with—and it's not easy making friends with new people—you decide to give it a try. *How do you feel about doing that?*

On Saturday, you get up at your normal 9:30, ask Dad if he'll make pancakes (with chocolate chips, of course), then walk down to the new house. *How are you feeling as you approach the door?*

You knock, and the new kid answers the door. After you introduce yourselves, he asks you to come in and see his baseball card collection. As he walks down the hallway, you notice he limps. Plus, his left foot is a little curved in.

Though the kid seems normal in every other way, his walk obviously isn't.

Questions to Think On

• *What are you thinking?*

• *What are you going to tell your friends about him?*

• *Will you play with him at school?*

• *What would be the good parts or bad parts about being his friend?*

What Does God Have to Say?

Enjoy the company of ordinary folks.   **Romans 12:13, LB**

Do not forget to entertain strangers, for by so doing some people have entertained angels without knowing it.

Hebrews 13:2

Offer hospitality to one another without grumbling.

1 Peter 4:9

2 ■ Buried Treasure

What If...

Recess is your favorite time of day and today you can't wait to get out and run around.

While playing on the big sawdust field, you spot something glistening in the sun. You walk over, look down, and what do you know, *it's a...*

No, it's not a quarter, it's a fifty-cent piece! Wow, you don't see many of them these days. You're sure it must be part of some kid's lunch money.

Your friends gather around you, call you "lucky" and then go back to playing. No one mentions turning it in to the office. They all expect you to keep it.

You put it in your pocket, but while you're playing several things go through your head: *Is some kid going to have to skip lunch today? What if it was from a week ago? What would I want someone to do if it was my money?*

As recess ends and you head back inside, that fifty-cent piece feels pretty good in your pocket.

Questions to Think On

• *What's your first reaction about what you should do with the money?*

- *What would you want someone else to do if it were you who lost the money?*

- *Is this a test or a gift? Did God give the money to you, or did he allow you to find it so you'd wonder what's right to do?*

- *What do you think the reward would be for turning it in?* (after your child says "money," say, "Besides money.")

What Does God Have to Say?

You shall not steal.   Exodus 20:15

He who has been stealing must steal no longer.
                                                  Ephesians 4:28

3 ■ Phone Phrustrations

What If...

You just walked in the door from work. You had a tough day, plus it took you almost an hour to get home because of an accident that clogged traffic. You're bushed. All you want to do is eat dinner and take it easy the rest of the night.

You change your clothes and sit down for dinner. During the prayer, the phone rings. You finish praying, then quickly get up to answer it.

It's a phone solicitor saying he's going to be in the neighborhood the next day and asking if you'd like a special deal on cleaning two rooms and a hallway–plus an estimate on the rest of the house. *What would you say?*

After getting off the phone, you go back to the table and start digging in. Two minutes later, the phone rings again.

This time it's an insurance salesperson. She asks if you'd like a free comparison of her company's rates with your own. *Now what would you say?*

Back at the table, you continue to eat your slightly luke-warm meal. The phone rings. By now you've had it! You say, "Let it ring." After the twelfth ring, you get up and walk quickly to the noisy beast. "Hello!" you say.

This time it's a real estate salesman asking if you're look-ing to sell your house... or know anyone who is. By this time you're really frustrated!

Questions to Think On

- *What would you say?*
- *Would you be tempted to lie? (Be honest.)*
- *How well do you think you handle frustrating situations when you're tired?*
- *Is fatigue a good reason to quit acting like a Christian?*

What Does God Have to Say?

But the fruit of the Spirit is love, joy, peace, patience, kind-ness, goodness, faithfulness, gentleness and self-control. Against such things there is no law.   Galatians 5:22–23

Do not let any unwholesome talk come out of your mouths, but only what is helpful for building others up according to their needs, that it may benefit those who listen.   Ephesians 4:29

4 ▪ The Family That Forgot to Say It

What If...

This is what happened at our house:

It was the same routine every day. The Flemming mom and dad got up at 6:30 A.M. At 7:30, they awoke their two children. "Good morning," they said. "It's time to get ready for school."

Matt and Mary got up, changed into their school clothes, ate breakfast and left for school. Dad and Mom went off to work in their separate cars. At 3:30, Mom came home from her job. As Matt and Mary arrived in the house, there was no warm greeting, only a snack.

"Time to do your homework," Mom said. "Then you can watch TV until dinner."

Dad arrived home at 6:00, and immediately dinner was served. But no one talked much besides saying, "Pass the salad, please."

After dinner it was more TV and then time for bed.

"Brush your teeth," Dad said. "I don't want to spend all of our money on dentist bills."

Matt and Mary obediently brushed their teeth, put on their pajamas and went to bed. An hour later, Mom and Dad went to bed, too.

This same routine happened day after day, week after week, month after month.

Questions to Think On

• *Name five things that are missing from this family.*
• *What do you think is the biggest thing they're missing?*

- *How do you feel when Mom and Dad don't say "I love you?" How do you think we feel when we don't hear it from you?*
- *How does God say "I love you" to us?*
- *What would it be like if you never heard God say he loved you?*

What Does God Have to Say?

How great is the love the Father has lavished on us, that we should be called children of God! And that is what we are!   1 John 3:1

This is how God showed his love among us: he sent his one and only Son into the world that we might live through him. This is love: not that we loved God, but that he loved us and sent his Son as an atoning sacrifice for our sins.   1 John 4:9–10

5 ■ Sticks and Stones...

What If...

Your Sunday school class is planning a Saturday hike up in the mountains. Though you don't know the kids in your class very well, you are actually looking forward to it. Neither Mom nor Dad can go, so it is sort of a day to be on your own.

When you arrive at the church to head up into the hills, you look for someone to hang out with. You know the names of most of the kids but you haven't really spent much time with them outside of class.

Three older kids you normally get along with get into the bus last, so you follow them in, hoping you can sit next to them. They head for the back of the bus and sprawl out on the back seat like they are going to take a nap.

"Could I sit with you?" you ask.

"I don't know if there's enough room. Hey, where'd you get that T-shirt?" one of them asks.

"I think my mom got it at the Christian bookstore."

"Hey, what do you think of someone who wears a T-shirt that says 'Apostle Paul's Travel Service' on it?"

"And I suppose your mom cut your hair, too?" another says.

Hmmm. You hadn't expected anyone to say stuff like this. Maybe they're having a bad day.

"Hey, sit down," one of the adult leaders says.

As you sit down, you suddenly get a bad feeling about this. You think you probably should have taken one of the open seats at the front of the bus. As the ride progresses, you know your feelings were right. For the rest of the forty-five-minute trip, these "friends" don't let up. Every time you open your mouth to defend yourself, they find another way to put you down. Needless to say, it's a very long trip.

Questions to Think On

- *Have you ever been put down before? How did it make you feel?*

- *Have you ever put someone else down? Why? Did you think about how it made the other person feel?*

- *How could you handle a situation like this?*

- *Mom and Dad: Why do you think people put others down? What are they trying to accomplish?*

What Does God Have to Say?

Better a patient man than a warrior, a man who controls his temper than one who takes a city.   Proverbs 16:32

A man's wisdom gives him patience; it is to his glory to overlook an offense.   Proverbs 19:11

6 ■ The Eyes Have It

What If...

It's Thursday. One more school day until the weekend! All of a sudden, your teacher announces you'll be having a pop quiz that you haven't studied for.

A quiz! you think. Since you haven't even looked at your books, there's no way you'll do well. The girl next to you pulls out some paper and says, "I've got this one aced. I've been studying all week." She's the smartest kid in class. She aces *every* test.

You pull out your paper and pencil, listening carefully as the teacher reads the first question. When your neighbor starts writing, your eyes take a quick glance at her paper. She finishes writing down her answer before you can even think of what to put.

As the teacher asks the second question, you know this test is going to get ugly unless you think quickly.

Questions to Think On

- *What would you do if the teacher turned her back?*
- *What would most of your classmates do in this situation?*
- *If you knew you wouldn't get caught, would you look on your neighbor's paper... just this once?*

- *Mom and Dad: What would you want your child to do in this situation? Why?*
- *What would you have done in the same situation back when you were in school?*

What Does God Have to Say?
The Lord abhors dishonest scales, but accurate weights are his delight.   Proverbs 11:1

Blessed are they who maintain justice, who constantly do what is right.   Psalm 106:3

7 ■ Who, Me?

What If...
It's the Wednesday before Thanksgiving. You're walking home from school thinking, *Four days of freedom! Four days to eat turkey, watch TV, do stuff with friends, sleep in, stay up a little later. Yes!*

When you get home, you toss your backpack into your room and head into the kitchen for a snack. Mom is already getting food together for Thanksgiving Day. It's cold outside, but the house is warm. Dad will be home soon and, since he's also got four days off, you know he'll be in a good mood–plus, Mom says he's bringing home pizza so she doesn't have to cook. No school, time off, warm house... and PIZZA!! It just doesn't get any better than this!

After pizza, out comes the Monopoly game. You haven't played in months, and Dad's acting like he can beat everyone. Just as you sit down to start the game, the phone rings. Surprisingly, it's for you. Your best friend from church is calling.

"Hey, what are you doing?"

"Just getting ready to play Monopoly," you reply. "How about you?"

"Well, my family and I are doing something really different for Thanksgiving this year and I wanted to see if you could come with us."

"I don't know, Mom's got everything all planned out. What are you doing?"

"We're getting up early tomorrow and going down to the mission to help serve homeless people their Thanksgiving meal."

"You're joking," you say. "Why?"

"Well, Dad arranged it. He said we needed to do something more meaningful this year. I can't believe we're not staying home to eat and goof off. But I'm actually looking forward to it, and I wanted to know, well, if you want to go with me for the day. I think it's going to be kinda fun."

You're stuck. You don't know what to say. All week you've been looking forward to just hanging out with your family. Instead of answering no, you say, "I doubt my folks will let me, but let me ask and call you back."

Questions to Think On

- *If we say, "It's up to you," what would be your first response?*
- *Is there any way doing this could be fun?*
- *Is there any way this could be a bad experience?*
- *What would you do?*
- *Mom and Dad: If your child asked to help serve others on Thanksgiving Day, what would you say?*

What Does God Have to Say?

Not so with you. Instead, whoever wants to become great among you must be your servant, and whoever wants to be first must be your slave—just as the Son of Man did not come to be served, but to serve, and to give his life as a ransom for many.   Matthew 20:26–28

For you know the grace of our Lord Jesus Christ, that though he was rich, yet for your sakes he became poor, so that you through his poverty might become rich.

2 Corinthians 8:9

8 ■ When the Doorbell Rings

What If...

It's a Sunday afternoon and the family car has pulled into the driveway at home. You took the family out for brunch after church and it's almost 2:00. After changing clothes, everyone quickly heads in different directions. Dad, you trudge off to the garage to work on the car. The brakes have been squeaking a lot lately, so you're pulling off the tires and checking the pads. Mom, you go to the spare bedroom to work on a few craft projects you haven't had time to get to. The older sister gets on the phone to talk with her best friend. The youngest brother heads downstairs to play. And the middle child stays in his room because it's a disaster area from having a friend over the day before. From the looks of it, it could be an all-day job.

Dad, you see it first through the garage window—the police car that stops next to the curb by our home. You watch as the officer gets out of her vehicle and heads up the walk to our front door. Wiping the black, greasy dirt from your hands, you head inside.

The doorbell rings.

Mom, you saw the patrol car, too, and you've beat Dad to the door. You don't have a good feeling about this. *Why would a police officer be coming to our house on a Sunday afternoon?* you wonder.

After introducing herself, the officer asks if she can come in for a moment. As she enters the house, all three kids arrive in the entry way to see what's going on.

"We've been trying to reach you all morning and early afternoon," she says. "When we finally got a busy signal, we realized someone must be home." Everyone looks at the older sister.

"I haven't been on *that* long," she says.

"I'm afraid there's a problem," the officer continues. "Mrs. Smith, your father's been in a pretty bad auto accident. He's at Mercy Hospital. It happened this morning about 9:15. He was able to give us your number before they wheeled him into surgery. He said you were the only family he had in town. I have to tell you, it doesn't look good. We'd like you to come to the hospital right away."

Questions to Think On

- *Mom, what would be going through your mind? What would be the first five things you would do?*

- *Dad, what would be going through your mind? What would be the first five things you would do?*

- *Have either of you faced a situation like this? Do you know anyone who has?*

- *Each person responds to bad news differently. Are there any specific ways Christians should respond when hearing news of this nature?*

- *How would you react if it was one of us kids in the hospital instead of a parent?*

What Does God Have to Say?

Be strong and courageous. Do not be terrified; do not be discouraged, for the Lord your God will be with you wherever you go. Joshua 1:9

And we know that in all things God works for the good of those who love him, who have been called according to his purpose. Romans 8:28

9 ■ Is a Half-Truth Better than No Truth?

What If...

It's Friday after school and you've spent a long week trying to keep up with your homework. You don't have any over the weekend and all you want to do is relax. After you throw your backpack into your closet, Mom reminds you that you've put off practicing your saxophone all week.

"I know I promised to do it after school today," you tell her, "but it's been a long week. Can't I just do it this weekend?"

"I knew you'd try to put it off again," she says. "Yesterday you begged me to let you wait until today so you could watch your shows, promising that you'd get it done today after school."

"But Mom, it's Friday, and I have the whole weekend!

Don't you trust me enough to get it done over the next two days?"

"Trust has nothing to do with it. You promised me yesterday that you'd get it done after school today. Now, are you going to do what you said, or do we just take the sax back to the music shop?

"I've got to go to the store for about half an hour," she continued. "I expect you to practice the whole time I'm gone. If you don't, you can just forget about TV tonight."

"Fine. I'll practice."

As Mom heads out the door, you pick up your sax and start to play. Your older brother is downstairs watching one of your favorite after-school shows. You play a few more notes, then lay your sax on your bed and sit on the stairs so you can see the TV. For the next twenty-five minutes, you watch the rest of the show. Just as the show ends you race back up to your room and start playing.

After Mom has finished putting away the groceries, she comes into your room. "How's it going?" she asks.

"Fine."

"Have you been able to get through your lessons?"

"Yes, Mom. I've been through this lesson before." (*A true statement since you have practiced this piece a number of times.*)

"Well, do you feel like you know it?"

"I'm getting there, Mom," you say. (*Again, another true statement.*)

"I appreciate you practicing while I was gone."

"Sure. No problem." (*She didn't say, "I appreciate you practicing the whole time I was gone."*)

Questions to Think On

- *Since it's fairly clear that you didn't, technically, lie to mom, do you have anything to feel guilty for?*

- *Leaving out parts of the truth is a well-known way to get out of taking responsibility for something wrong that you've done. How do you feel about doing this if you don't get caught?*
- *If you know that you may get punished for not following through or for telling only a partial truth, what are you more likely to do: take the punishment, or try to get away with something?*

What Does God Have to Say?

Buy the truth and do not sell it.   Proverbs 23:23

He whose walk is blameless and who does what is right-eous, who speaks the truth from his heart and has no slander on his tongue, who does his neighbor no wrong and casts no slur on his fellow man, who despises a vile man but honors those who fear the Lord, who keeps his oath even when it hurts, who lends his money without usury and does not accept a bribe against the innocent. He who does these things will never be shaken.

Psalm 15:2-5

10 ■ The Shopping Mall Caper

What If...

Our family has just arrived at the local mall. You can't wait to look around one of your favorite stores. There's a sweater you've been wanting, and you've saved up your allowance to get it.

As you enter the store, you notice four teenagers taking clothes into the side room to try on. After finding a couple of sweaters that might fit, you head in to the changing area yourself. While you're trying on the clothes you hear this conversation:

"All you have to do is put your jeans on over the shorts, and they'll never find out."

"Yeah, but won't it look kinda bulky?"

"What you do is hold the other clothes you brought in here over your pants. They don't look anyway."

"That's what you do for pants," says another voice, "but how about this sweatshirt? One sweatshirt over another looks pretty fishy."

"Do I have to tell you everything? What you do is leave the extra clothes you brought in here and head straight for the exit. We'll keep the saleslady busy by giving her back the stuff we don't take. Then it's on to the next store!"

As you finish trying on your second sweater, you laugh to yourself. These teens are stealing clothes. They're pretty clever, actually. *They'll probably get away with it, too,* you think.

Questions to Think On

- *What would be the first thing you would think if you overheard such a conversation?*
- *Name four things you could do.*
- *Which are you most likely to do?*
- *What are the possible drawbacks of telling the salespeople what was going on?*
- *What are the possible benefits of letting them know of these kids' plans?*

What Does God Have to Say?

For we cannot do anything against the truth, but only for the truth.   **2 Corinthians 13:8**

Anyone, then, who knows the good he ought to do and doesn't do it, sins. **James 4:17**

11 ▪ A NOTEworthy Difference

What If...

You really love playing the trumpet. In fact, since you picked it up in fourth grade, you have improved a lot. Though your parents sometimes have to remind you to practice, for the most part you don't mind taking thirty minutes or more a day to do your scales and practice assigned pieces. You carry your trumpet to school proudly, knowing you are the best.

When it comes to performing, every eye is on you. You play with more skill than anyone on any other instrument. You've performed not only at school talent shows and band concerts, but you even got to play in last year's Christmas program at church.

And this year you will perform a solo!

Yeah, you are at the top. That is, until *she* moves into the district.

She is Bonnie Williams, a girl who transferred in from another state when her dad switched jobs. Bonnie has been playing a variety of horns since second grade. Not only can she play the trumpet better than you, she can also handle the trombone, alto sax and flute!

The band instructor sees how good she is at trumpet and lets the two of you play side by side. The instructor thinks the competition will be good for you.

There is no mistaking that Bonnie is good; even better than you. While you'll still get to do the solo at church, you're no longer king of the hill at your school when it comes to music.

It's bad enough that Bonnie begins to play first chair–and gets the solos that you used to get. But what makes it worse is her personality. She is nice to everyone. Instead of having a big head and thinking she is God's gift to music, she becomes friends with many of *your* friends. She even tries to be friendly to you.

Questions to Think On

- *If this happened to you, how would you feel?*
- *What would you do?*

    a.. Practice harder so you could catch up to Bonnie's level

    b. Feel like there was no use trying to get better as long as she was around and decrease your practice time

    c. Talk to your parents and band teacher about quitting

    d. Make friends with her and find out her secrets

- *Has there ever been a time when you envied the talent someone else had in something you liked to do?*
- *Mom and Dad: Was there ever a time when you envied someone else? How did you respond?*

What Does God Have to Say?

Be devoted to one another in brotherly love. Honor one another above yourselves.   **Romans 12:10**

Do nothing out of selfish ambition or vain conceit, but in humility consider others better than yourselves.
                                                        Philippians 2:3

12 ■ The Herd Gives the Word

What If...

Summer is great! No school, no homework, no getting up or going to bed early. The problem is some of the time you drive Mom crazy. She's trying to get stuff done, but you're bouncing off the walls.

One day, a girlfriend calls and says that she and some friends are going to the mall theaters to see a movie and want to know if you can come. Putting the receiver down, you run to check with Mom. She asks who's going to be there. After you tell her, she wonders what type of movie you'll be seeing. Since a few of the girls are from your church, you're sure it'll be G-rated. Mom says you'd better check.

Getting back on the phone you ask what movies are playing. Your friend names a few of them. After you tell her that you could probably only see the G-rated one, she says she's sure the girls will want to see that one anyway.

You run to tell Mom the news and she gives her OK.

Though Mom doesn't like to just drop you off at the theater, she's in a hurry to get some shopping done before she has to pick you up. You walk to the window and pay the matinee rate for the G-rated film and enter the lobby. You quickly spot the other girls who are standing in line to get popcorn. That's when one of the girls has a suggestion.

"You know, we can go into any theater we want with these tickets. They don't check. Let's hit that one," she says, pointing to an R-rated movie poster.

One of the girls speaks up. "No, my mom would kill me if I saw that one."

You breathe a sigh of relief.

Then she says, "But she probably wouldn't care if we

went in that one," pointing to a PG-13 movie poster.
All of the girls agree that's the film to see.

Questions to Think On

- *What are your choices?*
- *What would your first response be? (Be honest!)*
- *What's more important at this point:*
  a. *Going into the movie and telling Mom afterward you didn't think she'd mind (knowing that you'd probably blow your chances to go to movies unattended later)*

  OR

  b. *Telling the girls that if they go into that one you'll have to watch the other one by yourself (since Mom's not home to come pick you up)*
- *Mom or Dad: In your opinion, how important is being able to trust your child? What will your response be when that trust is broken?*

What Does God Have to Say?

From heaven the Lord looks down and sees all mankind; from his dwelling place he watches all who live on earth—he who forms the hearts of all, who considers everything they do.   **Psalm 33:13-15**

Nothing in all creation is hidden from God's sight. Everything is uncovered and laid bare before the eyes of him to whom we must give account.   **Hebrews 4:13**

13 ■ The Listening Type?

What If...

You are twelve again and living with your parents. You have just entered junior high and you enjoy getting older and becoming more independent. The only problem is you need your parents' permission to do a lot of things.

For the following situations, answer these two questions:
1. What would your parents say about this? Why?
2. How do you feel about their advice?

a. Going to co-ed dances or parties
b. Spending all day with a friend in the wilderness (though not too far from your home)
c. Watching movies that have a secular edge
d. Talking to the opposite sex on the phone or "going with" someone
e. Frustration with church events, groups or activities
f. Wanting to stay up later or stay out later with friends
g. Choosing classes
h. Choosing friends
i. Any other situations you can think of

Questions to Think On

- *Were you the type to learn from other people's mistakes, or did you have to learn the hard way?*

- *In what situations do you want me to come to you and obey your advice?*

- *In what situations do you want me to come to you and at least listen to your advice?*

- *What will you do if I don't listen to your advice and I do what I want?*

- *What concerns you most about me growing up?*

What Does God Have to Say?

If any of you lacks wisdom, he should ask God, who gives generously to all without finding fault, and it will be given to him. James 1:5

A wise son brings joy to his father, but a foolish son grief to his mother. Proverbs 10:1

14 ■ The Accident

What If...

You and your sister both like music... *a lot!* You each have your own set of albums that you like listening to.

The problem, from your point of view, is she has a better stereo than you. Hers has two speakers, an AM/FM radio, a double cassette deck, and a CD player. She got it for Christmas last year. It was a big present, true, but she didn't get much else. You, on the other hand, have an older cassette player Dad used to use in his office. It works OK with cassettes, but it doesn't even have a radio.

You have asked to borrow her stereo on a number of occasions, but it's still too new. She doesn't even want to take it out of her room. Well, one day when she is staying late at school, you want to listen to one of her CDs. Dad is at work, and Mom is on an errand that will take about an hour. You think there won't be any harm in bringing your sister's stereo into your room for a while. After all, you know how to operate it, and this way, you can do a little homework while listening to music.

Everything goes pretty well. The music plays at a "reasonable level" (as Dad would say), and no one is home to see what you are doing.

After the first CD, you want to play one of your cassettes. You put the tape in and try to shut the door. The tape won't go all the way in, so you push harder. You hear a "crack," so you pull out the tape. It looks fine. Then you notice you are trying to put it in the wrong way. You turn it around, put it in, close the door, and press "play." A few muffled sounds come out of the stereo, but then it goes silent. Pressing "eject" and pulling out the cassette, you see that the brown tape has come completely out of the cassette casing. Though it is crinkled together, you are able to use a pencil to wind the tape back into its holder. You try another tape and it does the same thing!

This is really bad news. You suddenly realize you've done something to the tape player. Quickly unplugging the stereo, you put everything back in place in your sister's room. *No one will know I did anything,* you think.

To make a long story short, your sister soon realizes her tape deck is busted and she confronts you. Though you deny it the first time, when Dad gets involved you tell the whole story.

Questions to Think On

- *Though it was an accident, what would you do to make things right?*
- *Should you be punished for what you did, both breaking the cassette player and then denying it?*
- *What would you want to happen if your little brother or sister did something like this to something you valued?*

- *Can you think of a way something like this could have been avoided?*

What Does God Have to Say?

Do not repay anyone evil for evil. Be careful to do what is right in the eyes of everybody. If it is possible, as far as it depends on you, live at peace with everyone.

Romans 12:17–18

Now we pray to God that you will not do anything wrong. Not that people will see that we have stood the test but that you will do what is right even though we may seem to have failed.   **2 Corinthians 13:7**

15 ■ Close Friends?

What If...

You have three friends with whom you spend all of your time at school–and after. The whole school year you've been inseparable. Whenever you're on the playground at recess, all four of you are doing something: soccer, football, swinging from the monkey bars, making up imaginary games, all sorts of stuff.

As you're heading home from school one day with two of these friends, they start talking about the friend who isn't there.

"He's getting to be a real dweeb," says one.

"I know, he's saying stupid stuff to girls, and all he talks about is sports," says the other.

"Who are you talking about?" you say.

"Tim, of course. Haven't you been listening to all of the dumb stuff he's been saying lately?"

"No, like what?" you question.

"Like talking about girls all the time and wanting to go chase them. He even suggested we call up girls and hang up on them after they come to the phone. He's a jerk."

"Plus, he thinks he's really hot in sports. We've talked it over. What do you think, is it time to quit playing with him?"

"You mean, just ignore him, like he's not even there? Not call him anymore or go over to his house?"

"Yeah," they both say at the same time.

"Wait a minute. Tim's been our friend for a long time. Have you even talked to him about what he's doing?"

"Well...."

"I say we need to give the guy a chance. Maybe we can all talk to him and tell him where he's messing up. I think he'll listen."

"I don't... not at all. He's too stuck on himself. I say let's leave him in the dust."

"I can't believe you guys are thinking this way," you say. "Doesn't the guy deserve a second chance? Wouldn't you want to be told something if it were you acting weird?"

"Maybe, but it's too late. I can hardly even stand being around the guy."

"And maybe *you* need to decide what group you're going to be in," your other friend says.

"Maybe I do."

Questions to Think On

- *Have you ever had to choose between friends? What did you do?*
- *How important is loyalty in a friendship?*

- *If you were the guy the other kids were talking about, what would you want them to do: tell you how they feel, or just ignore you?*

- *Can you remember a time when the friends of Jesus had to choose between loyalty to him or loyalty to the world?*

What Does God Have to Say?

A friend loves at all times, and a brother is born for adversity.

Proverbs 17:17

A man of many companions may come to ruin, but there is a friend who sticks closer than a brother.

Proverbs 18:24

16 ■ Bored to Tears!

What If...

Our family attends church regularly. In fact, we're the church *and* Sunday school variety. While Mom and Dad hit the adult Sunday school class, you go to yours. You've been doing this for years and it really hasn't been all that bad. But this year... well, let's just say the teacher hasn't been able to put much time into making the class creative. She does her best, but in truth, the class is boring.

Now, you've sat through boring Sunday school classes before–but not for three straight months! You're getting tired of it and you've been complaining to us. We're sympathetic, but there's not much we can do. We've never taught your grade before and are locked into being discussion leaders in our own class for another six months.

Another problem is many of your friends don't like the class either. Several have quit coming and others only come once in a while. You don't even want to get up on Sunday mornings. You've told us a number of times you wish you could quit, but with our commitment to our class, we've said it's not possible. You suggest we talk to the pastor and tell him what's going on, but we say the teacher is probably doing her best and you should "tough it out."

After another boring Sunday, you announce to us that you hate church and you think it's time you got to decide for yourself whether or not you want to go. We can see how frustrated you are, but we don't budge. "Church and Sunday school are too important for us to miss," we say. "We'll just have to think of another option."

Questions to Think On

- *What other options are there?*
- *How can prayer help?*
- *Would it help or hurt to talk with the pastor or the Christian Education director?*
- *What makes a good Sunday school class?*
- *What can you do to make this class better?*

What Does God Have to Say?

Do not be anxious about anything, but in everything, by prayer and petition, with thanksgiving, present your requests to God. **Philippians 4:6**

Children, obey your parents in the Lord, for this is right. "Honor your father and mother"—which is the first commandment with a promise—"that it may go well with you and that you may enjoy long life on the earth."

Ephesians 6:1-3

17 ■ Thrifty, Cheap Or...

What If...

It's the Saturday before Mother's Day. Dad comes into your room and asks if you've bought or made anything for Mom. After giving him a blank stare, you say, "For what?"

"For Mother's Day tomorrow. Don't you remember?"

"Oh, yes, Mother's Day," you reply. "Not yet... but... I'm going to the mall later with some friends. I'll pick something up then."

"Do you have enough money?" he asks.

"Well... that depends on what I get her. How nice a present does it have to be?"

"Listen," he says in that serious tone you've heard before, "your mom works pretty hard around here taking care of all of us. I think she deserves something nice from you. How much money do you have?"

After checking, you tell him five dollars.

Dad says, "Five dollars! You can barely buy a card with that. I'll tell you what. I'll *loan* you twenty dollars. You can pay me back by doing a few extra chores over the next two months. Get her something nice, OK?"

"Right, Dad. Umm... any suggestions?"

"Well, she likes flowers, perfume, and then there's that craft stuff she never seems to have enough of. Be creative. Ask your friends."

Taking the money from Dad, you promise to bring back something nice.

As you walk through the stores, you see some things you'd like for yourself. You think, *There must be something nice and cheap I can get Mom. Then I'll have enough to get a couple of those posters I've wanted.*

You find a card and pick up a small Precious Moments figurine at Hallmark. Together they cost only $9.54! Now you have enough to buy those posters.

Questions to Think On

- *If this actually did occur, what would be your problem?* (Selfishness? Greed?)
- *In your own honest opinion of yourself, is there anything you feel you're selfish in?*
- *When you think of a selfish person, what comes to mind?*
- *Why is it sometimes hard to be unselfish, even when you want to be?*
- *What are some ways to work on being a more unselfish person?*

What Does God Have to Say?

A greedy man brings trouble to his family, but he who hates bribes will live.   Proverbs 15:27

The sluggard's craving will be the death of him, because his hands refuse to work. All day long he craves for more, but the righteous give without sparing.   Proverbs 21:25–26

18 ■ More Excuses than Time

What If...

Dad, you're a busy man.

You've been working long hours lately, not to mention coaching your daughter's soccer team, attempting to catch up on the yard work, leading a small group once a week with other adults from the church, and being a good husband and father. It's not easy being a dad.

As usual, you and Mom make sure we're off to church on time every Sunday. Most of the time we make it at least after the announcements and before the singing.

One Sunday we get to church, sing the songs, give the offering, then settle in to hear what God tells the pastor to say. Our pastor is a good teacher and even has a way of making his sermons interesting for kids my age. *(Hey, remember, this is "what if.")*

The pastor starts telling our congregation about how busy he is being our leader, being a husband and father, and trying to have a close relationship with God (the same kind of problem that you have). He admits that a while ago, he only read the Bible if he was studying for the sermon. He goes on to talk about a commitment he made a few months back to get into God's Word as often as possible. "It's not every day yet," he says, "but I'm getting close, and it's made a huge difference in the way I look at things."

Finally, he mentions a few helpful hints on how busy people can still read the Bible so they can become closer to God.

Questions to Think On (Dad *and* Mom can answer these questions)

- *Have you ever had a time when you were really consistent in reading your Bible? How did that make you feel about your relationship with God?*
- *When you are busy, is it tougher to read on a consistent basis?*
- *Is reading the Bible something important in your life? Why should it be important in my life?*
- *How often would you like to read the Bible? How can I help remind you?*

What Does God Have to Say?

The prudent see danger and take refuge, but the simple keep going and suffer for it.   Proverbs 27:12

Consequently, faith comes from hearing the message, and the message is heard through the word of Christ.

Romans 10:17

19 ■ Pair Pressure

What If...

There are always a few guys at school who like the girls. They talk about them, write notes to them, call them on the phone, and hang out at the mall hoping to *see* them.

Up until this year of school, you haven't paid much attention to it. You had more important things to think about. It's not that you didn't notice the girls; you were just never "brave" enough to do any of that stuff.

About halfway through the school year you hear from a friend that this girl likes you. It brings a smile to your face, but again, what are you going to do about it? Well, your friend tells a few other friends that you like her. You don't appreciate this blabbermouth saying this, but it gives you some attention from the popular crowd. For some reason, having a "girlfriend" puts you in a whole new category at school. And you've hardly talked to her yet!

Well, the rumors continue to fly, and suddenly someone puts a note in your hand. It's from the girl! She says she really likes you and would like to skate with you at the all-school skating party next Monday. Again, you smile.

A bunch of guys are standing around when the note is delivered, and now they *really* start in on you. They're certain you have a girlfriend.

Later that evening, you begin to think what happened during the day. You certainly like all of the extra attention you're getting, and you don't mind the idea of starting a friendship with this girl... but you're not sure if you're ready for a girlfriend. The problem is, if you write her a note or tell her you're not that interested, everyone will think you're chicken.

Questions to Think On

- *How could you have avoided this dilemma?*
- *What are you inclined to do: play along for a few days until people forget about it, or let everyone know the next day that you're not that interested?*
- *Mom and Dad: Did you ever feel pressured to "pair up" with someone when you weren't ready?*
- *What are your rules on such things? What do you think your son should do?*

What Does God Have to Say?

He who gets wisdom loves his soul; he who cherishes understanding prospers.   **Proverbs 19:8**

Do not conform any longer to the pattern of this world, but be transformed by the renewing of your mind. Then you will be able to test and approve what God's will is–his good, pleasing and perfect will.   **Romans 12:2**

20 ■ How Good Is Your Word?

What If...

It's Sunday afternoon and you just arrived home from church. The weather doesn't look too promising and there's not much on the tube. Dad comes to the rescue for a while by getting out the Scrabble game and keeping it lively. That kills an hour and a half. But even you know you can't let him entertain you all day.

Time for Plan B. You go to your room, grab a book and start reading. After about half an hour, your eyes get heavy and you fall fast asleep... for an hour! Mom wakes you up with an offer for an afternoon snack. Hey, that's a no-brainer.

It's still only late afternoon. After pestering your little brother for a while, you head down the street to see what a friend is doing. Not home. So you decide to walk down to the school playground to see if there's anything happening down there. Surprisingly, it's deserted. The clouds must have kept everyone away.

By the time you walk in the door back at home you're going crazy with boredom. But of course, Mom has a great suggestion: "A few chores will help pass the time."

Good ol' Mom! Always one to come to the rescue.

After you're done sweeping, raking, and vacuuming the car, it's dinner time. That's when you hear the best news of the day.

"You know how you all have been wanting to see that movie at the two-dollar theater?" Dad says.

Everyone's eyes light up.

"Well, it's been kind of a boring day. Why don't we jump in the car and try to catch the early evening show?" he says.

Fantabulous!

While Dad finishes up the dishes and you're getting ready, the phone rings. Mom says it's for you, but to make it quick.

"Are you still coming over tonight?" asks the voice on the other end.

"Coming over? Tonight? What do you mean?" you say in a surprised tone.

"Don't you remember you told me as we were leaving school Friday that you'd come over Sunday night and help me with our science homework? Well, I'm ready for some help, and my mom said she'd pick you up."

"Oh, yeah. Now I remember. Well...

Questions to Think On

- *What do you think you would say? Why?*
- *Have you ever had to choose between keeping your word and doing something you really wanted to do? What did you do?*
- *How important is it to you that other people keep their word with you?*
- *What do you see as a potential solution to this situation?*
- *Mom and Dad: What would you recommend your child do?*

What Does God Have to Say?

The Lord detests lying lips, but he delights in men who are truthful.   Proverbs 12:22

Who is going to harm you if you are eager to do good?

1 Peter 3:13

21 ■ How to Knock Shock Jocks

What If...

Mom gets a part-time job for a couple of weeks, but it means that you can't come directly home after school. Instead, Mom makes arrangements with Jill's mom to have you go over to her house every day until about 5:15. Then you can ride your bike home.

Jill is a good friend from school, though not your best friend. Her family doesn't attend church.

Normally when you get to her house, you have a quick snack and then go and do your homework. This arrangement actually works out well. Since there are no distractions like there are at your own home, you're able to get all your work done. That way you have your evenings free.

At the beginning of the second week, you get to her house, eat something and do your homework as usual. But this day you don't have much to do, so you're left with about an hour to kill. Jill turns on the radio and starts channel surfing down the dial. She goes quickly by a couple of your favorite stations and lands on 1555 AM, KJNK.

You've never sat and listened to this station before because you've heard about it from your friends at school (and your parents wouldn't let you anyway). As the DJ rambles on and on, you can see why they call the station K-Junk. About every other word out of this guy's mouth is either a swear word or a dirty joke about some ethnic group. Jill is laughing and having a good time listening, and you... well, some of what he's saying does *seem* pretty funny, but the hard rock music that's playing between all the verbal trash isn't the style you like.

Questions to Think On

- *Since not everyone shares your values about what to listen to (or watch), what can you do to protect yourself when something you don't appreciate is going on around you?*
- *What do you think is the best way to know whether something you're listening to or watching is a good idea?*
- *Have you ever heard of the word "discernment?" What do you think it means?*
- *Mom and Dad: Why is learning to discern good from evil so important?*

What Does God Have to Say?

Apply your heart to instruction and your ears to words of knowledge.   Proverbs 23:12

For this people's heart has become calloused; they hardly hear with their ears, and they have closed their eyes. Otherwise they might see with their eyes, hear with their ears, understand with their hearts and turn, and I would heal them.   Matthew 13:15–16

22 ■ Avoiding the Root of All...

What If...

In order to get you to do things, we have to motivate you properly. And what motivates you the most (much of the time) is money.

To get you to read during the summer we pay you a dollar or two a book (depending on how thick it is).

During the school year, whenever you get an A in a class, we give you three dollars!

And then, of course, you don't get your weekly allowance until you do your chores.

Plus, you always try to do extra work for more money. If the cars need washing and vacuuming, you negotiate with us on how much you should get if you do the work. Ditto with raking leaves, sweeping, dusting, and so on.

It's not that you are an absolute greed freak; it's just, well, you like to have money to spend. And what do you spend it on? Posters, music, candy, clothes, sometimes presents for others. At least three or four times a week you can be found in your room counting your money.

Questions to Think On

- *Do you think it would be unusual for a family or a kid to act this way?*

- *Would you say a kid like this is greedy, or just learning to appreciate money?*

- *We know that money isn't evil, but the "love of money" is. Has loving a possession ever caused you to tune out other things that are important in life?*

- *Mom and Dad: How tempting is it for you to put possessions above other priorities in life? How do you fight that temptation?*

What Does God Have to Say?

No one can serve two masters. Either he will hate the one and love the other, or he will be devoted to the one and despise the other. You cannot serve both God and money.

Matthew 6:24

For the love of money is a root of all kinds of evil. Some people, eager for money, have wandered from the faith and pierced themselves with many griefs.   1 Timothy 6:10

23 ■ Watch Your Yap

What If...

Our church has just finished its Sunday evening service. Along with singing and a message, it included a short business meeting. Though I was bored out of my skull, we sat through it. I noticed, Dad, that you and Mom were looking at each other and whispering in each other's ears. The meeting lasted only about fifteen minutes, but it seemed like an eternity to kids.

Now that it's over we head down the aisle toward the door. On the way out I hear you say something to one of your church friends.

"I don't care how the elders voted," you say. "This is something that can get a lot of people ticked off. The elder board had no right making that type of decision without asking the whole congregation first."

The other guy just nods. I give Mom a look and run off to the car.

On the drive home, you are still fuming.

"I'm going to call the pastor tonight. What they're talking about is ridiculous."

"Dear," Mom says, "don't you think you should think and pray about this first? After all, they're the ones who had all of the information."

"Well, then I want to see it!" you bark back. "I get so tired of the same people making the same stupid decisions without consulting folks like us who have been in the church for years. We ought to have more of a say. And what's the pastor doing in all of this? He must know there are going to be a lot of us who will be mad about it."

"Perhaps we should talk about this later, dear," Mom says while looking back at us kids in the back seat.

"Oh... yeah. Sorry."

Questions to Think On

- *Do you think it's right to criticize other adults in front of kids?*
- *When do polite discussions turn the corner and become accusations?*
- *How would Jesus handle disputes between Christians?*
- *Do you know that I'm watching you like a hawk and learning how to respond to situations by how I see you respond?*

What Does God Have to Say?

He who guards his mouth and his tongue keeps himself from calamity.   Proverbs 21:23

We all stumble in many ways. If anyone is never at fault in what he says, he is a perfect man, able to keep his whole body in check.   James 3:2

24 ■ The Winning Edge

What If...

You're a basketball player for your school's sixth-grade team. The team is pretty good and you get to play a lot. The reason: you're a good passer, and the coach likes having guards who can get the ball to the big guys. You don't shoot a lot–unless you're wide open. Quite a few fans show up to your games.

This game has been a tough one. Your opponents are trying everything to win, even leaving some of their weaker players on the bench so the regulars can get more time. Though your coach wants to beat the other team, he doesn't stoop to making players ride the pines just to win... usually.

The buzzer ends the third quarter and your team is down by six. Things definitely don't look good. Your coach takes you and a few other starters out and puts in the second-stringers–just like always. Two minutes later, your team is down by ten! It looks like there's no hope. The next whistle a minute later, however, the coach puts the regulars back in. It's a little early to go back in, but you sense he wants to see if you can make a comeback.

As soon as you go in you steal the ball and go all the way for a lay-up. The next time down they take the ball, shoot and miss. Bringing the ball up court, you spot one of your best shooters in the corner at the three-point line. You fire him a perfect pass, he sets, he shoots... swish! Down by five with three minutes to go.

The other team takes it down the court quickly and gets an easy lay-up. Down seven again. One of the other guards brings the ball down and sees you breaking for the basket. He gives you a bounce pass and you stop and pop. It hits the glass and goes in. Down five.

They inbound the ball and you steal it again. As you head toward the basket, the opponent who threw the bad pass comes hard at you. You take one dribble to your right and lay it in just as he hacks your arm. Sinking the free throw, you're only down by two with a minute and a half left. That's when the other team tries to stall. They pass the ball around without trying to score. Everyone is playing good defense, though, and you know they can't hold onto the ball forever. Finally, one of their players panics and takes a bad shot.

With fifteen seconds left you dribble the ball up court looking for your three-point shooter. He's covered. Dribbling to your left, you lob the ball into the center, hoping he can make a move and get an easy shot to tie the game. Seven seconds. Immediately, three guys cover him so he kicks the ball back out to you. Glancing at the clock, then the rim, you let the ball fly from behind the three-point line. It hits the back of the rim… goes straight up in the air… and through the net. A three-pointer! Your team wins by one!

In case you weren't counting, you scored ten points and had one assist in the last four minutes! Everyone runs up to you to give you high-fives. The coach gives you a big hug and lifts you off the ground. Mom and Dad are clapping and screaming like high schoolers.

The next day in school, everyone has heard about the great game you played and comes up to congratulate you.

Questions to Think On

- *There's nothing wrong with playing well and being congratulated. But sometimes too much attention over something done well can give a person a big head. How are you going to deal with all the attention?*

- *What do you think pride is? Can you have too much of it?*
- *What could you do to stay (not just act) humble?*
- *Feeling good about your accomplishments is important, but have you ever known people who make sure everyone recognizes them after they do something good? What do you think of these people?*
- *Mom and Dad: What's the best way to keep from becoming too proud?*

What Does God Have to Say?

Let another praise you, and not your own mouth; someone else, and not your own lips.   **Proverbs 27:2**

For by the grace given me I say to every one of you: Do not think of yourself more highly than you ought, but rather think of yourself with sober judgment, in accordance with the measure of faith God has given you.

Romans 12:3

25 ■ Some Things Just Aren't Funny

What If...

You're having a great time with your friends on the playground on a warm summer evening. You were bored, so you called them up and told them to meet you there. So far, you've played basketball, wall ball, and you just finished finding out who can jump the farthest in the long jump pit.

Everyone has worked up a sweat, so you head off to the drinking fountain. That's when the guys start telling jokes.

It starts out fairly innocent. That is, "knock-knock" jokes and a few others.

"What's purple and conquered the world?" one guy asks.

"Alexander the Grape," you say (Dad has told that one before).

"Ok, what's black and dangerous?" you fire back.

Hmmmmm.

No one has the answer. You've stumped them.

"A crow with a machine gun!"

Everyone moans.

"Hey, guys," Bobby says. "My brother told me a bunch of jokes he heard in junior high."

He starts telling "jokes" about another race, but he refers to them by using a word you're not allowed to use.

It's a stupid joke, but everyone except you cracks up. Another guy starts telling a joke about female body parts. It's sort of funny, but you feel weird about laughing. Bobby starts in on a few more racial jokes, this time talking about a group of people who come from a different country.

You've never heard any of these jokes before. The more they go on, the worse they get.

Questions to Think On

- *Do you see any harm in telling "jokes" about other races or jokes that deal with sex?*

- *What are your choices about what you should do?*

- *What would happen if you said something and then walked away if they didn't stop?*

- *How could you change the subject?*

What Does God Have to Say?

Finally, brothers, whatever is true, whatever is noble, whatever is right, whatever is pure, whatever is lovely, whatever is admirable–if anything is excellent or praiseworthy–think about such things.   Philippians 4:8

Nor should there be obscenity, foolish talk or coarse joking, which are out of place, but rather thanksgiving.

Ephesians 5:4

26 ■ The Kid with No Boundries

What If...

"Do I have the dumbest sister in the history of sisters or what?" says the obnoxious eleven-year-old.

Both parents look at each other and the mom says, "Now, now. You shouldn't say things like that."

"Mom, get a life. You knows she's an airhead as well as I do. Are you sure she wasn't adopted? She can't be related to us."

"Why don't we forget about your sister for a while and go watch a video? Doesn't that sound fun?" the dad asks trying to change the subject.

"OK, but I get to pick which one we watch."

"Fine, whatever you say."

"What kind of movies are these?" the kid says. *"Old Yeller, The Wizard of Oz, 101 Dalmations.* Come *on,* Dad. You've got to be joking. Why can't you ever get good movies like *Wayne's World* or *The Nightmare Before Christmas?* I can't believe what a wimpy family this is."

"Would you like some snacks?" the mom asks as she comes into the room.

"Yeah, I'd like a Pepsi, a bag of potato chips and a few of those brownies you made today. Bring 'em to me."

"Don't you think it's a little close to dinner to be eating all of that food? The lasagna will be ready in about an hour. I was just thinking of a small snack like carrot sticks to tide you over."

"Mom, I'm hungry now! I don't want to wait. You asked if I wanted anything, and that's what I want. Now would you just bring it to me like I asked?"

"OK, dear. I'll be right back."

Questions to Think On

- *If you were a parent, how would you respond to a child who was as demanding and rude as this?*

- *Parents need to set TV-viewing boundaries so their children don't fill their minds with bad stuff. What do you think about the boundaries you've been given?*

- *Parents need to make eating boundaries so their children get the right nutrition. What do you think about the boundaries you've been given?*

- *Parents need to have boundaries to ensure that everyone speaks kindly to other family members. Do you understand why?*

What Does God Have to Say?

There is a way that seems right to a man, but in the end it leads to death.   **Proverbs 14:12**

The way of a fool seems right to him, but a wise man listens to advice.   **Proverbs 12:15**

27 ■ Tuning in to the Right God

What If...

You're watching TV early one Sunday morning. There's not much on besides religious programming, and you watch it as you get ready for church.

The first show you turn to has all of these young, happy, good-looking singers. The minister who comes on between songs talks a lot about God doing something miraculous in your life today.

Hmmmm, you think, *this doesn't resemble my church very much.* So you use the remote to switch stations.

The next show has an older guy sitting at his desk talking very slowly and deliberately. None of what he says makes much sense to you so, before you fall asleep, you switch to another show.

WHOA! Here's a guy who likes to shout. He's yelling and telling the camera how loving God is, but then he starts talking about the fires of hell. He says "There's only *one way* to get to the pearly gates... that's through Jesus Christ." He keeps screaming in a rhythmic fashion. Soon, his words seem to just run together.

Three stations, three different ways people are trying to explain who God is and what he wants. Then you start thinking about our own family and what we believe. Mom and Dad talk about having a close "relationship" with God through prayer and reading the Bible. We're good people, but not perfect.

Who's right?

Questions to Think On

- *As you grow older, you'll find out that there are many varieties of Christians. Plus, there are several types of churches that don't teach what your church teaches on who Jesus Christ is and how to get to heaven. How do you know which one is right?*

- *What do you think all Christian churches should have in common?*
- *What do you think God is really like?*
- *Mom and Dad: What do you believe about how to get to heaven and how to live and enjoy life here on earth?*

What Does God Have to Say?

In the past God spoke to our forefathers through the prophets at many times and in various ways, but in these last days he has spoken to us by his Son, whom he appointed heir of all things, and through whom he made the universe. The Son is the radiance of God's glory and the exact representation of his being, sustaining all things by his powerful word. After he had provided purification for sins, he sat down at the right hand of the Majesty in heaven.   Hebrews 1:1-3

Jesus answered, "I am the way and the truth and the life. No one comes to the Father except through me."

John 14:6

28 ■ The Mouth That Wouldn't Stop

What If...

Dad, your brother and his family are coming over for dinner this weekend. Because he lives in another city, you only get to see him once a month or so. You both have kids that are the same ages, so it's usually a pretty good time.

He arrives promptly at 3:00 P.M. on Sunday Immediately all the kids go outside to play, and your brother and his wife exchange greetings with you and Mom.

Going into the living room, both you and your brother suggest turning on the TV to watch some football. Mom and his wife stay in the kitchen to talk.

A couple of hours after having some snacks and soda, you have a great idea. Pizza! You both chip in and order enough for everyone–delivered. Since it's a nice day, we kids eat outside. All of the adults chow down while watching the game.

The conversation moves toward your other siblings.

"Have you been to Gwen's house lately?" your brother asks. "It's a mess. I was over there last weekend and it looked like a pigsty. I don't think she's cleaned her bathroom in about a year."

"No, I haven't been able to get over there in a while," you reply. "She's always has been a little organizationally impaired."

"To say the least," your brother says, butting in. "I know she's got it tough since her husband left her, but that doesn't mean she shouldn't try to be a productive part of society. She doesn't work, she just sits around watching TV all day."

"Hey, have you had a chance to play golf with Dan lately?" you say, trying to change the subject to your other brother.

"Oh, I'm worried about Dan," he says. "Last month when I was there it didn't sound too good between him and Karen. Real icy, if you know what I mean. You know, I don't think he's been taking the family to Sunday night services."

"That's funny," you say, "I spent a few hours with him last week, and things seemed great. I can read him pretty well. I don't think things are as bad as you think."

Questions to Think On

- *Gossip is hard to stop once it gets going. Would it be easy for you to change the subject if this type of talk started up, or do you sometimes like to hear it?*
- *When are you most tempted to gossip about someone?*
- *Someone once said, "It's not good to start talking about other people's problems if you can't be part of the solution." Do you agree or disagree with that?*
- *Why is gossip so bad?*

What Does God Have to Say?

A gossip betrays a confidence, but a trustworthy man keeps a secret.   Proverbs 11:13

A perverse man stirs up dissension, and a gossip separates close friends.   Proverbs 16:28

29 ■ She Changed the Rules

What If...

You're industrious like your older brother, always looking for ways to make money. You do your chores to get your allowance, and you're always asking Mom and Dad what you can do to earn some extra cash.

One day, your brother tells you he's going to give up mowing lawns to start a paper route. He wants to know if you'd like to take over a few of his regular customers.

"Would I?" you say. "That would be great!"

The following Saturday, your brother takes you around to several homes to introduce you. He says a lot of nice things about you to the owners (stuff he's never said to you before) and encourages them to try you out. They all agree.

Next, your brother tells you when and how to do each customer's lawn and, most importantly, lets you know how much you should expect from each one. You take notes and write down every detail.

The big day finally arrives. You have four houses to do and you'll be making thirty-five dollars! It takes you almost five hours to mow all four lawns (pushing your mower and carrying your gas can between each house), but it feels good to have it done. All the customers give you cash, and you note exactly how much they paid.

When you get back home, though, you see that you've only got thirty dollars instead of thirty-five. Checking your notes, you see that the elderly lady on the corner gave you five dollars less than she used to give your brother.

What gives? you think. *I did just as good a job as my brother did.*

You check with your brother, but he doesn't have an explanation for you.

Questions to Think On

- *What are some possible reasons why she would have paid you less?*
- *If you found out she deliberately paid you less, how would you feel?*
- *When you are treated unfairly, what is your first response?*
- *Mom and Dad: Talk about some of the things that are unfair in this world, and how you respond when they happen to you.*

What Does God Have to Say?

Let your gentleness be evident to all. The Lord is near.

Philippians 4:5

I have no one else like him, who takes a genuine interest in your welfare. For everyone looks out for his own interests, not those of Jesus Christ.   **Philippians 2:20–21**

30 ■ The Empty Chair

What If...

Each day it's the same faces. Thirty-two kids, all in their assigned seats. At the beginning of the school year it's fun, waiting to see who's in your class, but by Thanksgiving you're ready for a change.

It's another weekday morning as you're getting ready to head out the door.

"Anything happening in school these days that's new or fun?" Mom asks.

"Nope, same ol' thing," you say.

"Well, try to make it a good day anyway, OK?"

"OK, see you tonight."

Arriving at school, you walk into your classroom. Normally you sit next to Marilyn. She's a nice girl, though not exactly someone you'd play with at recess. But she minds her own business and is friendly.

Marilyn's been absent for a few days, and when you get to your seat, the one next to you is empty again. Karen, who sits on the other side of Marilyn, asks you if you've heard about her.

"Heard what?" you say.

"Heard that she has cancer or something, and she won't be back the rest of the school year," Karen says.

"No way. I don't believe that," you say. But instead of ignoring what she's said, you walk over to the teacher and ask her if she's heard anything about Marilyn. She says she has, but she wants to tell the whole class.

The bell rings to start the day, and your teacher goes through a few announcements. The last one is about Marilyn.

"Perhaps some of you have heard rumors about why Marilyn has been absent from school lately. I spoke with her mother last night, and it seems that Marilyn is sicker than they first thought. I can't give you all the details, but I can tell you it's a form of cancer. She'll be in the hospital for several weeks, and I'm sure she would appreciate a note or something from anyone who would write one."

Questions to Think On

* *Even though this girl isn't a good friend, would you write her a note, phone, or go visit her?*

* *If you were very sick, what would you want your classmates to do?*

* *Some people are too busy to think about or have compassion for others. Are you the type who genuinely cares about others, or are you too busy to think about it?*

* *Mom and Dad: Did you ever have a classmate who got this sick? Did you do anything?*

What Does God Have to Say?

I tell you the truth, anyone who gives you a cup of water in my name because you belong to Christ will certainly not lose his reward.   **Mark 9:41**

Let us not become weary in doing good, for at the proper time we will reap a harvest if we do not give up. Therefore, as we have opportunity, let us do good to all people, especially to those who belong to the family of believers.

Galatians 6:9–10

31 ■ Back Row High Jinx

What If...

Your Sunday school class is usually pretty fun because the teacher is young and lets you get away with a lot. Plus, many of your friends attend.

After that, however, comes church. Sometimes you can follow what's happening, but it seems like it's geared more for adults than kids. Because you're getting older, you ask us if it's OK to sit with your friends in the back. You promise not to make any noises and to pay attention. We look at each other with that *yeah, right* expression, but decide to give you a chance.

Your intentions are good as you sit with four of your friends. You really want this to work. After the singing, and during the offering, a couple of them start to laugh and snicker. It's not too loud, but we look back at you. Trying to keep your friends quiet, you smile and wave at us.

When the pastor starts talking, it gets a little out of control. Your friends write notes on the offering envelopes in the pews, whisper back and forth, ask you questions—try to get you to laugh and have a good time.

You didn't think it would be this hard to pay attention, but pretty soon you're doing everything they're doing. When the pastor's sermon is over, you realize you didn't hear a word of it. As the church empties, you see an adult tell Mom something. She looks over at you.

Questions to Think On

- *If she asks how things went, what would you say?*
- *What could you have done to keep your friends quiet?*
- *What will you do the next week?*
- *Mom and Dad: How can your child get more out of church?*

What Does God Have to Say?

Great is the Lord, and most worthy of praise, in the city of our God, his holy mountain.   Psalm 48:1

Let us not give up meeting together, as some are in the habit of doing, but let us encourage one another–and all the more as you see the Day approaching.

                                        Hebrews 10:25

32 ▪ Some Things are Immovable

What If...

It's Saturday morning–allowance day!

For three dollars a week, all you have to do is take out the garbage, empty the dishwasher, fold a few clothes, sweep the garage, do a little yard work and keep your room clean. Not a bad deal considering... considering that Mom and Dad could choose to not give you anything. We could decide that being part of the family means you do certain things whether you get paid or not. But we don't. We cough it up every week, just like clockwork.

This particular Saturday you're lying around watching TV when the phone rings. It's your best friend, Cody. He asks you if you want to go see a movie with him and his family today. You check with your Mom and she says that would be fine.

"She said yes," you tell Cody. "What time will you be by to pick me up?"

"Noon," he says. "See you then."

You race to your room to check the cash supply. You can find only a dollar in change. *Gotta quit buying that candy after school,* you think.

Hey! It's Saturday. That means Dad owes you three dollars!

But when you find him, he says he'd love to give you the money but you haven't done your chores yet. Checking the clock, you see that it's 11:15. You've only got forty-five minutes to do all of your chores! Yikes! *Why did I lie around so much this morning!*

You're nearly certain that you can't get your chores done in that amount of time, so you plead your case with Dad.

"I promise that as soon as I get home from the movie, I'll get everything done. I'll even do some extra stuff for free."

"I know that seems like a good offer in your mind," he says, "but that's not the deal. We agreed that you would do your chores, then I'd give you the money.

"It's been like pulling teeth to get you to do them on time for the last three months. How do I know you'll actually do them? Your little brother has even tried to pick up the slack for you by filling in.

"I'm sorry, but the only choice I have is to stick to my guns. You've got to learn how to be responsible, so you may as well learn now. If you have them done, you'll get your three dollars. Not before. Not this time."

You hang your head as you walk away without saying a word.

Questions to Think On

- *Would you get busy on your chores, or would you just think they couldn't get done, so why hurry?*

- *By showing you're responsible in the little things, you show us we can trust you with other—often bigger—things to do. Is this a fair way to determine if you're ready to be trusted with more adult-type activities?*

- *How would you react if you were twenty minutes away from finishing your chores and your friends came by to pick you up, but Dad still wouldn't budge on the money, so you had to tell them you couldn't go?*

- *Mom and Dad: Talk about what you believe about the importance of your child learning responsibility.*

What Does God Have to Say?

The plans of the diligent lead to profit as surely as haste leads to poverty.   **Proverbs 21:5**

The sluggard craves and gets nothing, but the desires of the diligent are fully satisfied.   **Proverbs 13:4**

33 ■ How Much Is Enough?

What If...

Mom, you're a good employee. You've been with your company for many years. Your job is very fulfilling and has good benefits, but it doesn't pay that well. You're able to help with the family budget, but there's rarely enough for extras. Most of the time, your vacations are spent doing work around the house or relaxing with us kids.

Though many families you know don't have it as good as we do, you sometimes have this nagging feeling that you're missing out on something.

One Saturday morning you're out washing your car, a 1989 Ford. It's not a junker, but it doesn't compare with the cars of others in our neighborhood. As you're finishing up, one of the neighbors drives by in a brand-new minivan. She pulls into her driveway and motions for you to come over. She's a nice woman, but she likes to show off her new "toys" whenever she can. Acting interested isn't hard. You'd *love* a new car, but you know that you have to save to get braces for the kids, so the old car will have to do for a few more years.

That night, your brother calls you up and tells you about this new boat he bought. Well, it's not brand-new, but it is an eighteen-footer. He wants to know if you can get away for a few days of fishing. Explaining that you have to work some overtime this week, you decline.

The next morning at church, a friend from Sunday school corners you to tell you about the new hot tub her family got last week. She wants to know if you can come by later in the day to try it out. You say you'll see if you can break away.

It seems like everyone is getting new stuff... except you.

Questions to Think On

- *Have you ever felt like you just can't keep up with other families you know who are buying new stuff every year? How does that make you feel?*
- *When you think of the word contentment, what comes to mind?*

- *Do you feel like you are a contented person, or do you sometimes find yourself wishing for more "things?"*
- *What do you think is the secret of contentment?*

What Does God Have to Say?

A heart at peace gives life to the body, but envy rots the bones.   **Proverbs 14:30**

"Because he loves me," says the Lord, "I will rescue him; I will protect him, for he acknowledges my name. He will call upon me, and I will answer him; I will be with him in trouble, I will deliver him and honor him. With long life will I satisfy him and show him my salvation."

Psalm 91:14–16

34 ■ My Friend... the Spray Painter

What If...

You're riding your bike home from school. You had to take care of a few things after class, so it was nearly 4:30 before you left. The clouds are getting thicker and it's starting to get dark, but you know you have plenty of time to get home.

You live in a suburb close to the city. Almost every neighborhood there has a large brick wall that surrounds it. Lately, you've noticed a lot more graffiti (spray painting on the brick) than usual. You wonder if some gangs are moving into the area.

As you pass behind one group of homes, you see a guy next to one of the walls. He pulls something out of a bag and then starts spray painting some words. Stopping, you look hard to see what he's writing. Then the figure turns slightly and his face becomes more visible. He looks familiar!

Getting back on your bike, you ride closer, but slowly. You can't believe it. It's one of your good friends! He spots you and starts running, not knowing who you are. You take off fast on your bike and easily catch up to him. You yell to him who you are. He turns around to see, then slows down.

"It's just you," he says. "I thought it was someone who would try to narc on me."

"What are you doing spray painting that wall?" you say. "If you get caught you'll have to clean it up. Plus, your parents will probably ground you for a month. What are you thinking?"

"Ah, my parents don't care what I do. Besides, it doesn't look like they're going to be together that much longer anyway. My dad left really mad a couple of weeks ago and hasn't been back. I bet they end up divorced."

"What does your mom think?"

"All she does is cry and talk on the phone. We haven't talked much. I think she's avoiding the subject."

"So, why are you spray painting the walls? Is someone making you do it?"

"They don't *make* me do anything. They just say it would look cool to see the gang's name on the wall."

"You joined a *gang?*"

"Not yet, I'm still being looked at."

Questions to Think On

- *Though this situation may never happen to you, what would you do if you had a friend who was involved in gang activities?*
- *Why do you think this guy wants to join a gang?*

- *Should you ever tell on your friends to keep them out of worse trouble?*
- *What could be the drawbacks if you do? What are the potential benefits?*
- *Who would you talk to for help in making your decision?*

What Does God Have to Say?
The kisses of an enemy may be profuse, but faithful are the wounds of a friend. Proverbs 27:6

Above all, love each other deeply, because love covers over a multitude of sins. 1 Peter 4:8

35 ■ Trying to Measure Up

What If...
You've definitely noticed who the popular kids are at school. And as you get older–unfortunately–you notice them even more. Popular kids get most of the attention from others. They are noticed more by the opposite sex, teachers seem to like them more (usually), and they have lots of friends.

At your school, there's this girl named Erikka. She fits the popular mold perfectly. Not only does she have nice clothes, she also gets involved in class discussions–teachers love her. Even though she acts like a jerk sometimes, everyone wants to be friends with her. Why? Because if Erikka likes you, you're *in*.

Your wardrobe isn't even close to Erikka's, but you *do* have a pleasant personality and you're not a kiss-up to the teachers. Plus, it's easy for you to talk with guys; you know how to make them feel comfortable around you. You don't giggle or get embarrassed or do dumb stuff to try to get their attention. But for some reason, you aren't nearly as popular as Erikka, and that bugs you.

It's not easy being low on the totem pole. Sometimes you don't feel like you measure up; you even feel bad about yourself. All because when you compare yourself to Erikka... there's no comparison.

Questions to Think On

- *Have you ever envied (or wanted to be like) another person?*
- *Why do you think it's so tempting to compare yourself to others?*
- *When are you most easily fooled into thinking that you have to be like someone else to be liked more?*
- *Mom and Dad: When did you finally discover that it was a waste of time to compare yourself with other people?*

What Does God Have to Say?

Do not envy a violent man or choose any of his ways.

Proverbs 3:31

But if you harbor bitter envy and selfish ambition in your hearts, do not boast about it or deny the truth. Such "wisdom" does not come down from heaven but is earthly, unspiritual, of the devil.   **James 3:14–16**

36 ■ How to Get Clean

What If...

You and Mom decide to go to Target to do a little shopping. When you get there, you ask if you can just head for the toy section, where she can catch up with you later. She says that will be fine, so off you go.

Looking through toy sections at stores has always been one of your favorite parts about shopping. You know that when Mom shows up, you'll have about a half-dozen things you'll just *have* to get. She'll look at all of them very patiently while you make your case, but then she'll say, "Don't you have a birthday coming up?" or "Christmas is just around the corner, we'd better wait on buying new stuff." You'll act disappointed or mad when she says no, but it's quickly forgotten. It's a game you play that you rarely win, but it's still fun.

As you walk down the aisles, you spot a few toys that are out of their packages. You can't believe some kids actually open up toys to play with them, then leave them there. Just then, one of the store workers walks by.

"Excuse me," you say. "What do you do with all of these toys that are opened?"

"Well," he says, "if we can put them back in the packages, we try to do that. Sometimes we'll place all of the opened toys in a basket and sell them for half-price. Other times we just have to throw them away."

Throw them away, you think. *What a waste!*

Looking down, you see a small, unwrapped toy. You pick it up, telling yourself that this is probably one that they'd end up throwing away. All of a sudden you look around to see if anyone is watching. When the coast is clear, you put the toy in your pocket. A minute later, Mom pushes her cart around the corner. "Ready to go?" she asks.

"Ready," you say.

Getting home, you head to your room and shut the door. You can't believe how easy that was, just taking a toy that probably would have been thrown away.

A couple of weeks later you feel bad. You knew taking the toy was wrong, but it all happened so fast. Now you can't get it out of your mind. You decide you need to tell Mom what you did.

Questions to Think On

- *Have you ever done something that you felt guilty about after you did it? How did you get rid of the guilt?*
- *What do you think we would do if you "turned yourself in" like the person in this situation?*
- *What do you think you would have to do to stop feeling guilty about what you did?*
- *Mom and Dad: How do you get rid of your guilt when you do something wrong?*

What Does God Have to Say?

If we confess our sins, he is faithful and just and will forgive us our sins and purify us from all unrighteousness.

1 John 1:9

For as high as the heavens are above the earth, so great is his love for those who fear him; as far as the east is from the west, so far has he removed our transgressions from us.

As a father has compassion on his children, so the Lord has compassion on those who fear him.   Psalm 103:11–13

37 ■ "Umm, Excuse Me..."

What If...

It's Sunday morning and you're getting ready for church and Sunday school. Though you haven't *always* absolutely loved going to both, it's what our family does.

Getting out of the car, you know exactly where to go. It's been quite a while since Mom or Dad has had to take you to class.

Once inside, you see a few of your friends sitting next to each other, so you sit with them. Everyone starts talking about what they did the day before. One went to a water park, another saw a movie, another went to visit relatives. The teacher starts class right on time.

You've had this teacher for quite a while. He's stuck with your age group because he has a daughter in the class. Most of the time he makes class interesting, but then there are some Sundays...

This week, he's talking about Joshua and the battle of Jericho. You've heard the story a million times, but he's making it pretty interesting. You can tell he's done some homework on all of the particulars of the battle.

"Can you imagine what the people inside the city must have thought?" he says. "There were likely over three hundred thousand men marching around the city for six straight days. They didn't attack, they just marched. How would you have felt if you had been inside the city watching this happen?"

Everyone just sits there until one guy speaks up. "I'd feel pretty safe, actually. Weren't the walls real thick?"

"Very thick," the teacher says. "How would you have felt if you were one of the soldiers? You had to march around this huge city for six, then seven straight days. You weren't sure how you were going to win; all you had was the order of one guy, Joshua."

Again, not much response.

"Who knows," he continues, "if an earthquake hadn't brought down the walls, they might still be marching around."

That statement perks a few people up. You raise your hand. "Didn't God supernaturally bring down the walls after the big yell?"

"No, not really," he says. "You see, scientists have created an instrument that can identify where and when earthquakes occur. They can even measure an earthquake's magnitude. They have pinpointed that, during this time in the region of Jericho, there was an earthquake measuring 6.7 on the Richter scale. This would have been more than strong enough to bring down those walls."

You look around the room to see if the other kids really heard what you heard.

"In fact," he says, "though not all of the so-called miracles of the Old Testament can yet be explained, most have been found to be simply the results of nature."

Questions to Think On

- *If your teacher was saying things like this—that miracles weren't really acts of God, but simply coincidences of nature—what would you think?*

- *How do you normally respond when you disagree with an adult?*

- *What could you have said to disagree with this teacher without being disrespectful or making him look bad?*

- *Mom and Dad: When your children disagree with an adult, how would you want them to respond?*

What Does God Have to Say?

Submit yourselves for the Lord's sake to every authority instituted among men: whether to the king, as the supreme authority, or to governors, who are sent by him to punish those who do wrong and to commend those who do right.

1 Peter 2:13-14

When the queen of Sheba heard of Solomon's fame, she came to Jerusalem to test him with hard questions. Arriving with a very great caravan–with camels carrying spices, large quantities of gold, and precious stones–she came to Solomon and talked with him about all she had on her mind. Solomon answered all her questions; nothing was too hard for him to explain to her.

2 Chronicles 9:1-2

38 ■ The Unexpected Question

What If...

You're outside working in the yard while we kids are out riding bikes. You look around the neighborhood and see that there are a lot of folks outside doing yard work.

This is a good neighborhood, you think.

You know how important it is to try and share your faith with neighbors, but so far, you haven't had a lot of opportunities. Everyone always seems busy, and most of the time, you never even see them. They come home from work, press their electric garage-door openers, drive in and disappear until the next morning. The farthest you ever get with most of them is "Hi, how are you doin'?" Which always evokes a "Fine, how about you?"

The neighbors next door are a perfect example. You know the husband's and wife's names, but you're fairly certain they don't know yours. *How do you share your faith with people if you never talk to them and they can't even remember your name?* you think.

This day, you decide to take your hedge trimmers and walk over to start a conversation.

As you make small talk at first, the conversation goes from the weather to your jobs to the neighbor down the street who doesn't take care of his yard. You're wondering how to bring the topic around to spiritual things, but there doesn't seem to be an opportunity.

As the conversation starts to slow down, you look for a chance to make a graceful exit so you can return to your yard work. That's when you hear a question you weren't expecting.

"So what church do you go to?"

"Huh?" you say.

"I've noticed that every Sunday you head out fairly early. I assume you're all going to church. Which one do you attend?"

"First Evangelical over off of Maywood. Have you ever been there?"

"No, we don't go to church. It's our only morning to sleep in. I used to go when I was a kid, but it got too boring and all the people ever did was argue about the pastor. My parents finally had enough and quit. Being a kid, I didn't mind. Now when I see people heading off to church, I wonder if all churches are like ours was. Actually, sometimes I've even wondered why people would ever want to go at all."

Questions to Think On

- *How would you respond to this statement?*
- *Has anyone ever asked you why you go to church? What did you say?*
- *Have you ever had a bad experience with church so that you wondered if you should keep going?*
- *When I'm older, will I have a choice whether to go or not go to church?*

What Does God Have to Say?

I am not ashamed of the gospel, because it is the power of God for the salvation of everyone who believes: first for the Jew, then for the Gentile.   Romans 1:16

So do not be ashamed to testify about our Lord, or ashamed of me his prisoner. But join with me in suffering for the gospel, by the power of God.   2 Timothy 1:8

39 ■ Nice Interception

What If...

You class is usually pretty organized. When there is a disruption, the teacher deals with it right away.

It's nearing the end of the school year, however, and your teacher has become a little more lax. He'll often leave the class for a few minutes to go to the office, or he won't look up from his desk when there is noise during study hall.

On one particularly bright spring day, you're in the library with the rest of your classmates. Though the teacher isn't around, most kids are still doing their work. You heard a rumor during the first recess that Amanda likes Scott, but you haven't seen them together on the playground yet. To your knowledge, Amanda's never had a boyfriend.

You're minding your own business, studying away in the library. You have a final project on insects due in two days and you're going buggy trying to get it done. You've got three encyclopedias spread out in front of you and you are almost ready to put the finishing touches on the role of insect antennae. Suddenly, you hear some noises a few tables down, so you look up.

Amanda's trying to get something back from Lois. It looks like a piece of paper. Lois won't let go of it and Amanda is getting visibly mad. Lois sneaks it behind her back and hands it to Gary, who quickly hands it down to Paul, who gives it to Tami, who hands it to Abbey, who reaches across the table and gives it to you. You don't know what's going on, so you unfold the paper. It's a letter to Scott… from Amanda! You can see it's personal, and it says some things that would be really embarrassing to Amanda if you were to read it out loud. Which is what everyone wants you to do.

You're faced with a dilemma: read the note and everyone in the room will laugh, or give the note to Amanda and everyone will groan and think you're a jerk.

Questions to Think On

- *What would you do?*
- *Why do people laugh at others who are embarrassed or made to look stupid?*
- *If it was a note that you had written, would you care if someone read it so everyone could hear, or would you want to have it back?*

• *Giving someone a break won't always make you more popular, but it is the right thing to do. Why is doing the right thing sometimes tough to do?*

What Does God Have to Say?

Finally, all of you, live in harmony with one another; be sympathetic, love as brothers, be compassionate and humble.

1 Peter 3:8

This is what the Lord Almighty says: "Administer true justice; show mercy and compassion to one another."

Zechariah 7:9

40 ■ Remembering You Have It All

What If...

This is a typical day in your life:

From midnight to about 7:00 A.M. you sleep in your own room and nice, warm bed. The sheets are clean, a small light is left on all night, and your clock radio is on your nightstand.

When the alarm wakes you, you immediately put in a tape of your favorite radio series, *Adventures in Odyssey*. Looking through your drawers, you see about a dozen different outfits you could wear to school that day. You also have four different pairs of shoes to pick from.

You head to the kitchen for breakfast, where Dad is waiting and ready to fix you whatever you want. This morning you feel like Cream of Wheat. He goes to work without any complaint. "Do you want juice with that?" he asks. "Sure," you say as you gulp down the cereal.

When you finish, you put your homework into your backpack and climb into the car. The weather is bad, so Mom is taking you to school.

After a full day of classes, you come home to a snack and conversation. You don't know what life would be like without having Mom at home to talk to. Walking down the hallway toward your room to do your homework, you pass through the cozy house you've called home for many years. The floors are clean, pictures are on the wall... *this is a good place,* you think.

About 6:00 P.M., Mom calls everyone to dinner. Dad sits down, prays, and asks how everyone's day was as a nice hot meal is dished up.

After dinner you head downstairs to play a game or two before watching an hour or so of some of your favorite TV shows. During the second show, you're hungry so you head up to the kitchen to get some cereal. There are about ten choices staring you in the face, but only a couple with no sugar. *Oh well, Chex isn't so bad.*

When it's time to hit the hay, Dad comes in your room to pray with you and see if you want to talk. As you read a chapter from one of the dozens of books in your room, your eyes get heavy. You turn over and drift off to sleep.

Questions to Think On

- *Though no one's home life is exactly like this, many kids have something close to this type of life; a good one. What would come to your mind if you considered all that you've been given?*

- *If thankfulness was one of the things that came to your mind, whom would you thank?*

- *How often and in what ways would you say thanks?*

- *Mom and Dad: When you were little, did you appreciate what you'd been given or did you take it for granted? How would you like your child to communicate thankfulness?*

What Does God Have to Say?

Always giving thanks to God the Father for everything, in the name of our Lord Jesus Christ.　　**Ephesians 5:20**

Enter his gates with thanksgiving and his courts with praise; give thanks to him and praise his name. For the Lord is good and his love endures forever; his faithfulness continues through all generations.　　**Psalm 100:4–5**

41 ▪ The Overnighter

What If...

"It's going to be a blast," you tell your best friend on the phone. "First we meet at the church with our sleeping bags, pillows and pack, then we load up the vans and head out into the wilderness! It only takes about an hour, and when we get there all the leaders cook the food while the kids go exploring. We get to stay up as late as we want, eat s'mores, tell stories... you'll love it!"

Your friend is convinced and ready to go!

A week later you're at the church, loading up and heading out. Even if it's just an overnighter, it's as exciting as a week at camp.

After an hour in the van, you pull into the camp. Your friend gives you a look to say, *This place is perfect!*

"OK, let's put our stuff away and find out what's around here," you say.

"Campers! Campers!" the leader yells, trying to get everyone's attention. "We've got a lot of work to do before dinner, so we need everyone to pitch in. You six go with Mr. Maxwell. You've got the dinner detail. You four (pointing at you, your friend and two other campers) go with Mr. Abbott and start setting up the tents for the rest of us. It should take you until dinner time. You seven go find as much firewood as you can. We'll need it pretty soon 'cause it's getting dark. OK, let's get it done."

Your friend gives you that *I thought this was going to be a vacation* look.

"It wasn't like this last year," you say. "Last year the adults did everything and we just ran around."

Mr. Abbott overhears what you've said. "Yeah, but that wasn't any fun. You didn't learn anything. This year we're a team. And everyone's important. We've all got to help if we're going to get things done. Let's get to work."

Work?

Questions to Think On

- *How would you feel about having to pitch in to help get the camp ready?*
- *Do you pitch in at home to help around the house and yard?*
- *How is a family like a team? What would happen if one of the teammates didn't do his or her job?*
- *When you are asked to do things around the house, what is your first reaction? How could that get better?*

What Does God Have to Say?

For even when we were with you, we gave you this rule: "If a man will not work, he shall not eat." We hear that some among you are idle. They are not busy; they are busybodies. Such people we command and urge in the Lord Jesus Christ to settle down and earn the bread they eat.

2 Thessalonians 3:10–12

42 ■ Whom Will You Choose to Win?

What If...

"So, what would you kids like to do this Saturday?" Mom asks you and your sister. "Dad's going to be out of town and I've got a few extra hours. Let's all do something fun."

That sounds great to you. You've been racking your brain in school the past few weeks and doing homework every weekend. You're ready for a break.

"I know what I want to do," your sister says. "Go swimming and then to the miniature golf course."

"That sounds like fun to me," Mom says. "How about you?"

To you that sounds OK. But you'd much rather spend the day at the mall. You haven't bought any new CDs since before school started and there's a million more things to do there.

"I've got a better idea," you say. "Why don't we walk around the mall for a while, and eat lunch at the food court, then hit a movie?"

"Oh, the weather's going to be nice this weekend. Are you sure swimming and mini-golf don't sound better?" Mom says, with that *let's not disappoint your little sister* look.

You've got your heart set on the mall, seeing your friends, going shopping, hitting a movie... but you can see you're in a dilemma.

"Why don't you talk it over after dinner? Whatever you decide is fine with me," Mom says as she heads into the kitchen.

After the dishes are cleaned off the table, you call your little sister into your room. *It shouldn't be too tough getting her to come around,* you think.

She sits quietly while you make your case again for the mall. You're pretty convincing if you do say so yourself. You end by saying, "And I promise, next month we can all go swimming, OK?"

"But I want to go swimming now," she says in that whiny voice of hers. "I haven't been able to go swimming in months. I don't want to walk around a hot, crowded old mall for four hours, and there aren't any movies playing that I want to see."

Questions to Think On

- *What would you do or say next? Can you see any way to compromise?*

- *Though you have just as much right to do what you want as your sister does, what's really important here: getting your way or giving in and making her happy?*

- *Why is it so hard to be unselfish? If you gave in, would you try to have a good time, or would you mope around the whole afternoon?*

- *Mom and Dad: When did you begin to learn how important it is to think of others instead of yourself all the time?*

What Does God Have to Say?

Even a child is known by his actions, by whether his conduct is pure and right.   **Proverbs 20:11**

My son, if your heart is wise, then my heart will be glad; my inmost being will rejoice when your lips speak what is right.   **Proverbs 23:15–16**

43 ■ Layoff

What If...

Mom, you have been working at the same company for many years. It's been a good job because it's kept Dad from having to work a lot of overtime. Plus, the money has come in handy for summer vacations, braces and the holidays.

For months now you've been hearing rumors that your company is preparing to cut back on employees to save money. While a few people have been let go, you've been told that your job is secure. That's always good news, because the town you live in doesn't have many jobs for a person with your skills.

One Friday, just as you're getting ready to leave, your boss calls you into his office. He doesn't look happy, and you get that sick feeling in the bottom of your stomach.

"I'm afraid I have some bad news," he says in a low voice. "The company has made some further cutbacks. They told me to let people go based strictly on how long they've worked here. Though you've been here for quite a while, there are over fifty others who have been here longer. Your number just came up. I'm sorry."

Though you're shocked, you're not mad at your boss. You know it's not his fault. You thank him for being a good guy, then walk out.

Driving home, you don't know exactly how you're going to break it to the family. You realize what this type of setback means. The prospects of finding another job right away are pretty bleak.

When you walk in the door, we kids are watching TV while Dad is changing his clothes upstairs.

Questions to Think On

- *What would you do first when you arrived home?*
- *Have you ever faced this type of major disappointment before? How did you respond?*
- *On a scale of one to ten, how bad would this actually be on the "disaster" meter?*
- *How do you think God could use this for good?*

What Does God Have to Say?

God is not unjust; he will not forget your work and the love you have shown him as you have helped his people and continue to help them. We want each of you to show this same diligence to the very end, in order to make your hope sure. We do not want you to become lazy, but to imitate those who through faith and patience inherit what has been promised.   **Hebrews 6:10–12**

Through him you believe in God, who raised him from the dead and glorified him, and so your faith and hope are in God.   **1 Peter 1:21**

44 ■ On-Line Answers

What If...

You're a pretty good student in almost every subject—except math. When it comes to desiring to do homework in that subject, well, let's just say you'd rather do anything but that.

Unfortunately, of course, you can never get out of it. You've begged Dad to help you with it, secretly hoping he would just tell you the answers (which he did sometimes). Even Mom has been a help when you were stuck. But now, we say we'll help you do the problems, but you've got to get the answers yourself.

Panic sets in. Your brain just doesn't understand the material. You're afraid that if you don't do well on the homework, you won't get the five dollars we promise you for every A or B you get on your report card.

All of sudden, it comes to you.

I'll call Jerad and tell him I'm just checking my answers with his, you think. *I'll ask what he got, then say "That's what I got."*

A brilliant plan indeed. In fact, it works the first few nights. Jerad doesn't catch on to what you're doing. But we do. Every night after dinner, you've been escaping to our room to use the phone in private. Unfortunately, you forgot how funny it might look if you took your homework in there with you. After a few more days, Dad comes into your room before bedtime.

"Why are you taking your math homework into our bedroom with you every night when you say you're going to use the phone? You haven't been asking us for help on it lately. How are you doing in class?"

Questions to Think On

- *You've just been busted, but there is probably a way to skirt around the issue so you don't lie, but you don't tell him the whole truth. What would you do?*

- *Do you feel pressured from your parents in any way to get great grades?*

- *Is getting good grades more important than not cheating to do it?*

- *Mom and Dad: What would you rather have, a child who gets good grades by occasionally "fudging," or one who does his or her best while getting Cs and Ds—but who never cheats or fudges on homework or tests?*

What Does God Have to Say?

So then, brothers, stand firm and hold to the teachings we passed on to you, whether by word of mouth or by letter.

2 Thessalonians 2:15

Pray for us. We are sure that we have a clear conscience and desire to live honorably in every way.

Hebrews 13:18

45 ■ Rubbing It In

What If...

You're playing baseball against a team that you've always considered your archrival. The players are from another grade school in your area and you know a few of them. You've grown up playing against them... and you don't like them very much. In fact, the parents of the teams don't even like each other.

The other team beat you once already this year in a close game—on their field. The umpire made a few questionable calls that didn't go in your favor. But now you're ahead five to four in the top of the sixth. The other team has their last ups. If you can hold them, you'll win.

The first guy up lines a single to center field where you field it and throw it to second base. The next guy hits a grounder up the middle. Your shortstop knocks it down and flips the ball to second base to force the runner there. One out. On four straight pitches, the next guy up walks.

Runners on first and second, one out... and one of the team's best hitters is up. In the last game, he hit a double to knock in two runs and seal the win.

He takes one strike and swings at another. The next two pitches are balls. It's two-and-two as the runners take their lead. When the pitcher winds up, you see the runners break for second and third–trying a double steal. The batter smacks a line drive your direction, but you get a good jump on it. Running in and to your left, you stick your glove out across your body and... and... make an incredible catch! Keeping your balance, you see the guy that was on second is all the way to third. The shortstop is on second, waving his arms. You plant your foot and make a perfect throw to second before the runner gets back.

Double play! You win!!

Needless to say, you're mobbed by your teammates. Back at the dugout, as you're getting ready to give the other team a yell, you notice they're not going to give you one. Your team does it anyway, then lines up to shake the other team's hands. You can't wait to see the guy whose ball you caught.

Questions to Think On

- *Are you the type who might "rub it in," or would you do something else?*
- *When you think of the word sportsmanship, what comes to your mind?*
- *Is it ever OK not to be a good sport?*
- *Mom and Dad: What are your views on sportsmanship?*

What Does God Have to Say?

But he gives us more grace. That is why Scripture says:

"God opposes the proud but gives grace to the humble."

James 4:6

Though the Lord is on high, he looks upon the lowly, but the proud he knows from afar.   Psalm 138:6

46 ■ Taking the Fall for a Dirty Dog

What If...

When you got your dog a few years ago, you promised you'd take care of it. But now, just as we predicted, Mom and Dad do most of the work. Oh, we don't complain too much about it. We realize it comes with the territory of being a parent.

Even though you don't always have to feed Max, you still have to keep an eye on him. For the most part, Max stays in our yard, but sometimes he likes to get out and explore the neighborhood. When he does, he'll usually start digging in someone's flower bed. That's when you hear about it from us (because *we* hear about it from the neighbors). In fact, Dad has said that if Max tears up someone's flowers again, *you'll* be punished.

As you're heading up the hill toward home one day after school, you look toward our house and see that the gate to the fence has been left open.

"The dog!"

Immediately you start yelling out Max's name. After about the fourth yell, you see him running from the back of a neighbor's yard.

"Uh-oh."

The dog is wagging his tail a mile a minute and looks

happy–too happy–as you head toward him.

"What have you been up to?" you ask him (as if he'd tell you if he could).

Going around to the back of the house to investigate, you quickly spot the damage. The dog has completely dug up the vegetable garden. Lucky for you the neighbors aren't home. Re-planting as many vegetables as you can, you look around one last time and take your dog home– hoping no one saw what happened.

That night during dinner, the phone rings. Dad answers. It's the neighbor. Dad is silent for a minute, then turns around to look at you. Holding the phone on his chest, he says, "Did Max get out of the backyard today?"

Questions to Think On

- *If you knew you were going to be punished if you admitted the truth, what would you do?*
- *What do you think it means to "take responsibility"?*
- *Why is that so difficult sometimes?*
- *Besides taking responsibility, what are your options?*

What Does God Have to Say?

A false witness will not go unpunished, and he who pours out lies will perish.   **Proverbs 19:9**

A false witness will perish, and whoever listens to him will be destroyed forever.   **Proverbs 21:28**

47 ▪ Turning the Other...

What If...

It's Friday after school and the day is perfect for soccer. After getting Mom's permission to call a few friends and go down to the school to play, you grab your soccer ball and head out the door.

About fifteen minutes later there are eleven of you who have converged behind the junior high. One guy even brought four orange cones to make the corners of the field. You choose teams and start the game. It's great living in a neighborhood where so many like to play soccer.

After your team has scored a couple of goals, three older guys show up and announce that they'd like to play. Since you're playing six on five, it seems like a good idea. You know who the three guys are, but you're not exactly friends with them.

For about ten minutes the game goes well. There aren't any rough plays to argue about, so everyone's having fun. Your team gets ahead six to four. On the next kickoff, a couple of kids on the other team decide they're going to play with a little more "intensity." They push more and one of them even tries to trip everyone from behind. They get another goal, but the player who scored it clearly pushed your teammate away to make sure he had a clear shot. The next time down the field one of the older guys does the same thing—only harder. You see it clearly and rush in and say, "No way you're getting that goal, that was a push!"

The guy says, "I made that goal fair and square. Game tied."

Two or three others from your team rush in and say that it sure looked like a penalty. He starts yelling that it wasn't and says all of you are just being poor sports. No one on his team says a word while he continues to argue about the goal.

All of a sudden, one of your teammates declares, "You were pushing and tripping, no goal. Our free kick." Well, that does it. The other player is so worked up he runs and tackles the guy who said it. You run over to pull them apart. As you do, the player turns and gives you a hard punch in the stomach. He is older, though not bigger than you. His punch moved you back a little, but you think you could take him. He turns to you and says, "Let's go, wimp."

Questions to Think On

- *What are your choices at this point? What do you feel like doing?*
- *What is probably the best solution, considering all the potential consequences?*
- *If you fight, what are the possible benefits and drawbacks?*
- *If you back off, what are the possible benefits and drawbacks?*
- *Is there ever a time when you should fight, even if you're a Christian?*

What Does God Have to Say?

It is to a man's honor to avoid strife, but every fool is quick to quarrel.   **Proverbs 20:3**

You have heard that it was said, "Eye for eye, and tooth for tooth." But I tell you, Do not resist an evil person. If someone strikes you on the right cheek, turn to him the other also.   **Matthew 5:38–39**

48 ■ The Fifteen Dollar Dilemma

What If...

Mom, you're home with us kids on a hot summer morning. The weatherman predicts it will get up into the nineties. That means it will be miserable unless someone can think of a way to keep cool.

When we say "Water World," your eyes light up a little, but then you remember.

"It's expensive to spend a day at one of those places. What is it now, twenty-five dollars?"

"Not for me," I say. "I can still get in on kid's prices, since I'm only twelve. And so it's just ten dollars... I'll even pay half for me if we can go."

"That's twenty-five dollars for me, ten dollars for you, twenty-five dollars for your older brother, and ten dollars for your younger sister. Seventy dollars!"

"Well, call Dad, see what he says."

Your phone call doesn't get through. You've got to make this decision on your own.

I suppose I could use the VISA card, then have a garage sale in a couple of weeks to pay it off, you think.

"OK, we'll go... but we can't be spending a bunch of money on food. Not at those prices. All I've got is ten dollars, plus your five dollars. So let's get an assembly line going here and make some sandwiches we can eat on the way."

Forty-five minutes later, you're on your way, confident that Dad won't be too angry. Driving up, you remember that parking costs five dollars. *Now we're down to ten. Well, it's too late to back out now,* you think.

Climbing out of the car, we start following the masses to the line. After about ten minutes, we reach the front.

Scanning the board that lists the prices, you see it: "Adults $25. Kids 11 and under, $10."

Looking at me, you say, "I thought you said it was twelve and under for ten dollars."

"Oops."

Thinking quickly, you realize you could probably get away with saying I'm eleven. After all, you reason, my birthday was just a month ago.

Questions to Think On

- *Would you be (or have you ever been) tempted to get away with something like this?*
- *How do you feel after you fail to do the right thing?*
- *Have you ever had to go back to a business and make things right?*
- *Why do Christians sometimes struggle with doing what is right when it seems the answer is obvious?*

What Does God Have to Say?

Who may ascend the hill of the Lord? Who may stand in his holy place? He who has clean hands and pure heart, who does not lift up his soul to an idol or swear by what is false.　　　　　　　　　　　　　　**Psalm 24:3–4**

But the seed on good soil stands for those with a noble and good heart, who hear the word, retain it, and by persevering produce a crop.　　　　　　　　　　**Luke 8:15**

49 ■ Caught with Your Mouth Open

What If...

It's almost the last day of school and we tell you you can do something special to celebrate. You suggest a sleep-over with a bunch of girls from your class. We agree!

A few days before the end of the school year, you make your list: Amy, Susi, Lisa and Barb. *I'll start with those four, and then see if I need to invite more,* you think.

The next day you see Amy on the playground and ask her to come. She sounds pretty excited, but has to check with her parents first. It hits you that all of the girls are going to have to ask their folks, so you decide to invite the other girls by phone tonight.

That night after dinner, you make the calls. All three girls are excited about the idea and their parents say yes.

"We're going to have such a blast," you tell Barb. "What movies should we watch?"

"Let's talk to the other girls tomorrow before school and see what they say," Barb says. "They may have seen the movies you and I suggest."

"Good idea. See you tomorrow. Bye."

The next day you meet the other girls near the tetherball courts. Seeing Amy, you call her over.

"Well, what did your mom and dad say about the sleep-over? Can you come?"

"They said we're leaving early for vacation the next day, so I can't."

All of a sudden, Tiffany walks up. "Did I hear someone say sleep-over? What are you girls planning? Can I come?"

Tiffany is a girl that hardly anyone at school can stand. She thinks she could get any guy she wants to "go with" her. Most of the girls try to avoid her.

Amy blurts out, "Well, since I can't come to your sleep-over, you have room for one more. See ya."

Questions to Think On

- *What would you say if you had to make the decision?*
- *Would you be tempted to stretch the truth a little on what Mom might say?*
- *What is the worst that could happen if Tiffany came over? The best?*
- *Accepting someone into your group that you don't necessarily like isn't easy. How important is it for a Christian to accept others?*

What Does God Have to Say?

He has showed you, O man, what is good, And what does the Lord require of you? To act justly and to love mercy and to walk humbly with your God.   Micah 6:8

And the Lord's servant must not quarrel; instead, he must be kind to everyone, able to teach, not resentful. Those who oppose him he must gently instruct, in the hope that God will grant them repentance leading them to a knowledge of the truth, and that they will come to their senses and escape from the trap of the devil, who has taken them captive to do his will.   2 Timothy 2:24–26

50 ■ Getting Even

What If...

You and your younger brother get along pretty well most of the time. Yes, there are those occasional fights, but nothing too serious. Why do you get along so well? You have to sleep in the same room, that's why! If you didn't get along, you'd have killed each other by now.

Each of you has certain habits that tend to get on the other's nerves. Again, nothing serious. One's a neat freak, the other is "organizationally impaired." One likes the light on, the other doesn't. One likes silence when falling asleep, the other likes to have the radio on. You get the idea.

Lately, however, your brother drives you crazy. He has allergies and his nose is stopped up most of the time. Consequently, he must breathe through his mouth when he sleeps. He gives off a nasal sound that drives you up the wall. Though you know he can't help it, you're always trying new tricks to get him to stop: throwing a pillow on his head, shining a light in his face, whistling, stuff like that.

Finally, you just can't stand it anymore. One night after you've gone to bed, he falls asleep before you do. He's nasaling, and you've got your eyes wide open. Mom and Dad can't help. You're stuck! And you're also angry. Something has to be done!

Questions to Think On

• *What would you do to get back at him for all of the sleepless nights he's caused?*

• *Does getting even really make you even? Or does it just make you temporarily feel better?*

- *When you think of the phrase, "Do to others what you want them to do to you," what do you think?*
- *This is a tough situation. What are other situations you face where you'd rather get even with someone instead of being nice to them?*

What Does God Have to Say?

Do not judge, or you too will be judged. For in the same way you judge others, you will be judged, and with the measure you use, it will be measured to you.

Matthew 7:1-2

"Consider carefully what you hear," he continued. "With the measure you use, it will be measured to you–and even more."

Mark 4:24

51 ■ The Church Camp Dilemma

What If...

It's June, and almost the end of school. Every year our family plans our summer vacation around church camp. Camp is always a blast–the games, the archery, the cabins and food, even the music and speakers are good. You wouldn't miss it.

In the past, you've tried to get some school friends to go, but when their parents hear that it's a church camp, they're a little afraid of what that means. So far, you've never been able to attend with anyone besides your friends from church.

As your Sunday school teacher explains this year's camp, he also tells you to start praying about who God wants you to invite. "It's not just a camp for church kids. I really believe some of your friends who aren't attending a church would love it." He goes on to say more about camp being a great place for people to meet God and discover what he can do in their lives.

Immediately, you know who you should ask. A friend on your soccer team. She's also in your class. You know she would have a blast... if you could only convince her to go.

But... there's that problem of parents always saying no when they find out it's a church camp.

What if I tell them it's a church camp, but that we don't talk much about God, you think. *That would probably help her parents say yes.*

Questions to Think On

- *Have you ever been tempted to say something that isn't true in order for something good to happen?*
- *Do you think it's ever right not to tell the whole truth?*
- *If God wanted someone to go to camp, do you think he could get them to go without using deceptive methods?*
- *Mom and Dad: Why is total honesty always the best policy?*

What Does God Have to Say?

He whose walk is blameless and who does what is righteous, who speaks the truth from his heart.... He who does these things will never be shaken.   **Psalm 15:2, 5b**

"These are the things you are to do: Speak the truth to each other, and render true and sound judgment in your courts; do not plot evil against your neighbor, and do not love to swear falsely. I hate all this," declares the Lord.

Zechariah 8:16–17

52 ■ Pennies From Heaven

What If...

It's your birthday... your favorite time of the year. Not only does it mean you are one year older, but you will also score a lot of great presents from Mom and Dad and friends who come to your party. The best part about this day, however, will be when Mom gives you all of the birthday cards that come in from relatives.

Why? Because they all will have cash in them!

This year you turn ten, so that means that most people will put in ten dollars.

Sure enough, you load up on cool presents. And when Mom brings out the stack of cards she's been collecting from the mailman, you think for sure you have hit the jackpot. There turns out to be eighty-five dollars in them!

You write thank-you notes to everyone, and then you have the pleasant task of figuring out how to spend it all. *Should it be new clothes, some CDs, a pair of rollerblades, or a new putter for Dad?*

That's when Dad took you aside for "a little talk" about money. He says, "There are a million different things you can spend your money on, but there are only two ways to invest it.

"The first is by giving at least 10 percent back to the Lord. It doesn't matter where you give it; the Lord just doesn't want you to get too used to thinking all the money you get is yours. He knows it's important to not get too attached to things like money. Giving your money to good causes is a good way to remember just that.

"The second is by investing in your future. Again, 10 percent is a good round number. That means you give ten cents of every dollar back to yourself. You do that by putting it in a bank where it can collect interest."

Questions to Think On

- *Have you ever heard about the importance of giving and saving portions of the money God gives you? How do you feel about those two things?*
- *Which do you think will be tougher: giving to God or giving back to yourself? Why?*
- *Does God need your money, or do you need to give?*
- *Mom and Dad: Talk about your giving and saving habits.*

What Does God Have to Say?

In the house of the wise are stores of choice food and oil, but a foolish man devours all he has.　　　**Proverbs 21:20**

Each man should give what he has decided in his heart to give, not reluctantly or under compulsion, for God loves a cheerful giver.　　　**2 Corinthians 9:7**

53 ■ Two Ticked-Off Drivers

What If...

Driving isn't one of your favorite activities. When the traffic gets heavy or if the weather's bad, you tense up.

On one particular day you're taking us kids to a movie at one of the mall theaters. As you're going down the freeway in the left-hand lane, you see that you need to take the next off-ramp. You take a quick look in your rearview mirror and move abruptly into the right-hand lane. Just as you do, the driver moving up on the right gives a long honk. Then he changes lanes and comes up on your left. As you're moving into the exit lane you look over and he's yelling at you and shaking his fist.

"I'm sorry, it was an accident," you yell at the window though he can't possible hear you. "Chill out!"

When he sees you've yelled something back, the driver tries to get in behind you in order to follow you on the off-ramp.

Now you're angry... and a little scared.

Questions to Think On

- *If the other driver followed you all the way to the mall, what would you do?*
- *Though you're angry at how the driver responded to a mistake, what would be the best course of action to take?*
- *Have you ever become angry at someone for making a mistake on the road? How did you respond?*
- *To prevent an ugly situation or cool one down, what is the best course of action?*

What Does God Have to Say?

In your anger do not sin.   **Ephesians 4:26**

A patient man has great understanding, but a quick-tempered man displays folly.   **Proverbs 14:29**

54 ■ To the Rescue?

What If...

Ah, lunch time. Your favorite half hour.

As usual, the cafeteria is a madhouse. The kids who bring their lunch head for the milk line; the hot-lunchers get to stand and wait a little longer.

On this particular day, your class has arrived a little early. A younger grade is still ahead of you in line. As everyone crowds, some kids in your class notice a couple of overweight little kids with glasses. Since your classmates are just waiting in line, they figure they're entitled to some "entertainment." They immediately start in.

"Look, it's the Four Eyes twins," says one.

"And doesn't their hair look pretty all slicked back like that?" says another.

"I can see they haven't lost their baby fat yet, either. Are you sure you shouldn't just skip a few lunches so you can slim down?"

You look around for a teacher to come to the rescue, but they're all busy at the back of the line. As the kids from your class keep it up, one of the little kids tries to give it back. He actually gets in a few good lines. This gets some laughs and the older kids get mad—that's when the pushing starts.

"Oh yeah? Why don't we just skip lunch and go outside? We'll see how funny you are out there," an older kid says to the younger one.

The little guy keeps his mouth closed. He realizes he's said too much. The older guy doesn't like the silence and slugs him on the arm. It was a hard hit, and you could tell it must have hurt, but the younger kid doesn't move.

Now the older kid is really mad.

You look around and see there are no teachers nearby to break up the fight. It's up to you.

Questions to Think On
- *If the kids doing the teasing were a little bigger than you, what would you do?*
- *Have you ever come to someone's rescue before? Has anyone ever stuck up for you?*
- *Why do you think big kids pick on littler ones?*
- *Mom and Dad: Why do you think the strong pick on the weak?*

What Does God Have to Say?
Rescue the weak and needy; deliver them from the hand of the wicked.   **Psalm 82:4**

He who mocks the poor shows contempt for their Maker; whoever gloats over disaster will not go unpunished.
                                                      Proverbs 17:5

55 ■ Dad's Big Helper

What If...
It's been a long week for you–and Dad. You've had tons of homework, soccer practices, band rehearsals, and church on Wednesday. You haven't even watched TV all week!

Dad has been swamped beyond anything you can remember. He's at work even before you get up every morning and he's not home until you're just about ready to doze off to dreamland. A few of his co-workers are on vacation and the company has had hundreds more orders than usual, so he's had to fill in. It happens every year, but it's never been this bad.

Finally the week is over. Dad arrives home about 8:30 on Friday night. This time, you're still up. He comes in your room to catch up on the week with you. It's great to talk with him again. He asks you about your week, so you try to recount it as best you can. You ask him about his and he just gets this weary look on his face. He explains a little of what he's doing and says it doesn't look like it's going to slow down in the next couple of weeks, either.

Fortunately for you, your schedule *will* slow down! Next week will be a breeze compared to the last one.

After breakfast on Saturday morning Mom gives each kid a note from Dad. Here's what yours says:

Good morning! Sorry to leave a note, but I had to head to work early again. I really need your help this week around the house, especially in the yard. Mom's got a hectic week ahead, so I'd like you to take care of these things: weed the garden and the flower beds, clean the bathroom, wash Mom's car, straighten up your room, and get the toy area all in order. I know that's a lot, but with me being gone so much, I need you to pitch in. Thanks. Love, Dad

Wow! That's a lot of work!

Questions to Think On

- *What would you do if Dad really did give you an assignment that big?*
- *How do you feel about pitching in around the house?*
- *Growing up has a lot of benefits, but it also means accepting more responsibility. How do you think you'll respond to that?*
- *Mom and Dad: What are some signs that your child is growing up and becoming more responsible?*

What Does God Have to Say?

Don't let anyone look down on you because you are young, but set an example for the believers in speech, in life, in love, in faith and in purity.   1 Timothy 4:12

Do you see a man skilled in his work? He will serve before kings; he will not serve before obscure men.

Proverbs 22:29

56 ■ Packaged Treasures

What If...

Collecting sports cards is your favorite hobby. You love getting them, opening up the packages and seeing what treasures await within. Mostly you collect baseball and basketball cards, but lately you have been buying football and hockey cards, too. Your collection is incredible. You have boxes of cards you never look at anymore because they are full of "commons," plus you have notebooks full of "star" cards. Whenever a card show comes to town–and you have money to spend–you are there, buying and trading.

After school one day you stop by the local supermarket with a buddy before heading home. You have a couple of dollars in your pocket so you buy a few packs of Topps baseball cards. Your friend doesn't have any money. He also collects cards, though not nearly as many as you.

You open the packages and look through them carefully. No sense bending a corner in case you hit pay dirt.

In the first package you get a Frank Thomas. In the second one you get a Barry Bonds and a Ken Griffey, Jr.! Though you already have the Barry Bonds, the Griffey is a big find. The third pack is the best. You get the same Thomas and Griffey, plus a Jeff Bagwell and Greg Maddux!

Your friend is excited for you, but then he asks a question you didn't expect.

"Since you got an extra Griffey and Frank Thomas, do you think you could give them to me, or maybe I could trade you for them?"

Giving up a Griffey or Thomas is like giving him a dollar bill. Everything with either of their names on it is worth at least a buck.

Give them to him or trade… hmmmmmmm.

Questions to Think On

- *What would you do?*
- *Why is it so hard to give up something of worth?*
- *What do you think God thinks when we are generous to others?*
- *Are there people you can be generous with right now who would be happy if you gave them something of value?*

What Does God Have to Say?

A generous man will himself be blessed, for he shares his food with the poor.   Proverbs 22:9

In everything I did, I showed you that by this kind of hard work we must help the weak, remembering the words the Lord Jesus himself said: "It is more blessed to give than to receive."   Acts 20:35

57 ■ The Vicious Loudmouth

What If...

It's Wednesday, the night you go to Kids Club at your church. You play games, memorize verses and work your way through a Kids Club handbook that has a lot of Bible stuff in it. The leaders work pretty hard at making it fun for all the kids—and most of the time, it *is* fun.

But there is this one kid named Steve who drives you crazy. He always has to be the center of attention. He thinks he's Mr. Comedian and is always cutting other people down. Tonight during discussion time you raise your hand to answer a question, but you don't give the right answer and Steve starts in on you. Before the teacher can stop him, he nails you good—twice! The class erupts in laughter and you feel really stupid.

After Kids Club is over, you stay to talk to the leader about the upcoming day-hike. Dad said he would drive and you need to get a few more details for him. As you head out the door, the teacher notices that Steve has left his backpack. He asks you if you'd mind trying to catch him in the parking lot.

Swinging the backpack over your shoulder, you race up the stairs toward the parking lot to see if you can catch him before he leaves. A few thoughts run through your head about what you'd really like to do with the backpack, but you push them from your mind.

When you reach the parking lot, you head out into the pouring rain to see if you can find him. After a few minutes of looking into car windows, you conclude that Steve is gone. Now you're really mad. Not only did the guy make you look like a fool in class, but you're soaking wet, too.

What do I do now with the backpack? you think. *Hmmm. I*

could "accidentally" leave it out in the rain.

Questions to Think On
- *Would you be tempted to take revenge on Steve?*
- *When people do things to you that make you look or feel bad, do you try to get them back?*
- *Does getting someone back really make you feel better?*
- *Mom and Dad: Talk about revenge and if you think it's ever worth it.*

What Does God Have to Say?
But I tell you who hear me: Love your enemies, do good to those who hate you, bless those who curse you, pray for those who mistreat you.   Luke 6:27–28

Do not take revenge, my friends, but leave room for God's wrath, for it is written: "It is mine to avenge; I will repay," says the Lord.   Romans 12:19

58 ■ The Skeptical Neighbor

What If...

You are always looking for ways to get to know our neighbors better. Why? Though you don't see them as targets, you realize how important it is to live your faith in front of them—and perhaps even tell them about it if they ask.

One Saturday night you invite the Haydens over for dinner. They're an older couple and all of their children have left for college and jobs. Mr. Hayden has been nice about lending us his tools, and Mrs. Hayden was the only one to greet us when we moved into the neighborhood. (She even brought over some pumpkin bread.)

You pray for the meal, and after everyone has dished up and started eating, Mr. Hayden begins talking.

"You guys are churchgoers, aren't you?"

"We're Christians, Sam," you say. "Sometimes there's a difference."

"When we first got married we went to the church Miriam grew up in," Sam continues. "But you know what those church folk did? Over some little thing, they made life miserable for her dad. He was the greatest guy in the world. But what they did to him really tore him to pieces. I looked at that and said there's no way I'm going to let them do that to me. We quit going completely; haven't been back since."

"That's a tragic story, Sam. I've been a Christian for a long time and one thing's sure: Christians are humans who sometimes do really dumb things. I've been disappointed and let down by friends at church before—and I know it will happen again. That's why I look to God and the Bible and not to other sinful humans—like me—to tell me what God is like."

"I read the Bible once," Sam says while scooping another spoonful of mashed potatoes in his mouth. "I didn't understand most of it, and didn't agree with the rest. I'd like to believe, but I don't know why the Bible is so necessary. Can't someone just be a good person and believe what they want to believe about God?"

Questions to Think On
- *Why is the Bible so important?*
- *How would you answer Sam's last question?*

- *It seems that Sam is an honest doubter. How would you try to bring him along?*
- *At the end of the evening, what would you say to try to keep the conversation going for another time?*

What Does God Have to Say?

Be merciful to those who doubt.   Jude 22

But in your hearts set apart Christ as Lord. Always be prepared to give an answer to everyone who asks you to give the reason for the hope that you have. But do this with gentleness and respect.   1 Peter 3:15–16

59 ■ Christmas Expectations

What If...

It's getting close to Christmas and you've been giving us hints about what you want–a bike!

Not just any bike, of course. A red twelve-speed. Since you're getting older, you think you're ready for something bigger; something you can ride to visit a friend who lives a long way away. While at Sears last week, you even showed us the exact model you want. We smiled, looked at each other, but didn't make any promises.

"Things are pretty tight financially," we said. "I don't think we can pull it off this year."

Well, we've said stuff like that before just to throw you off the trail. You still think there's a good chance we'll get it for you.

Christmas morning finally arrives. You get up before anyone else and race out to the living room.

No bike.

You run to the garage to see if we've hidden it there.

No bike.

As you head back to the living room, Mom says, "Looking for the bike? Well, like I said, we just couldn't afford it. Sorry, honey."

The presents you do get are pretty good, but you're still disappointed the bike didn't come.

Later in the day a couple of friends call and tell you about the cool new bikes they got. They want to ride over to your house right now.

Questions to Think On

- *What would you be thinking if this really happened?*
- *Would you be jealous of your friends or happy for them? (Be honest.)*
- *Having your hopes let down isn't easy. Though we never promised a new bike, is there anything different we could have done so you wouldn't have been let down so hard?*
- *How are you going to act and what will you say when your friends come over?*

What Does God Have to Say?

Rejoice with those who rejoice; mourn with those who mourn. **Romans 12:15**

I have learned to be content whatever the circumstances. **Philippians 4:11b**

60 ▪ The Basketball Nightmare

What If...

You're one of eight players on your YMCA basketball team. This is only your second year of playing competitively, but you've picked it up fairly well. You can dribble with your right hand without looking, and can almost dribble left-handed. You're good at lay-ups and free throws, but not too hot on the shot from the side. As one of the guards who brings the ball down the court, you can usually get it to the forwards and center without throwing it away.

It's Saturday morning and you're playing another team. Today you're in the starting lineup. Though you were feeling good in warm-ups, the game isn't going too well. By the end of the first quarter, you've missed all three of your shots and the other team has stolen the ball from you twice. Plus, you've thrown the ball away once and dribbled it out of bounds another time. Not a good start.

Your team is down by seven as play begins in the second quarter. As you sit on the bench and cheer your teammates on, they make a comeback and tie the game at seventeen. With three minutes left in the quarter, the coach puts you back in. Your first pass is intercepted and the player goes for a lay-up. As you're inbounding the ball, your foot is on the line. Violation, other team's ball. They score again to go up by four. You begin to get a sick feeling in your stomach because you can't seem to do anything right. Your goal now is to make sure you don't touch the ball. The half ends after you miss two easy shots from inside the key.

Unfortunately, the second half gets worse. Every time you're out of the game, the team comes back. Every time you're in, you turn the ball over. In fact, you miss another four shots and turn the ball over five more times. You can see the frustration on the coach's and players'–and parents'–faces. Your team ends up losing by fifteen.

After the game the coach takes you aside and gently mentions a few things you need to work on. All of your teammates walk by while he's talking to you. You know you need his help, but you feel embarrassed.

Questions to Think On

- *Have you ever felt badly because you let others down by not measuring up?*
- *What do the words "being humbled" mean to you?*
- *Though it doesn't feel good to not do as well as you'd like, what can you learn from failing?*
- *Mom and Dad: Describe a time when you failed, how you felt, and what those around you said.*

What Does God Have to Say?

He who listens to a life-giving rebuke will be at home among the wise.   **Proverbs 15:31**

Before his downfall a man's heart is proud, but humility comes before honor.   **Proverbs 18:12**

61 ■ "I Can Take Care of Him, I Promise"

What If...

You have asked us for a pet for years. You can't understand why we won't get you a dog or something. As you get older, you keep asking us. Finally, we look at each other and say to you, "If we get you a pet, it's *your* pet. That means you must feed it, bathe it and take it out. Whatever it takes to take care of the animal, you have to do it."

After assuring us a hundred times you are old enough to do all that, we put the issue on hold. After a few weeks we say we really don't want a dog or cat in the house to get hair everywhere. That disappoints you, but we do have a point.

Two weeks later, you notice the rabbits in a pet shop at the mall. They look nice and the salesperson says that if you keep the bunny outdoors, you won't have to worry about hair or smell. *Perfect,* you think. *They can't shoot this idea down.*

Well, to make a long story short, we listen carefully to your argument and decide you *are* old enough to take care of the rabbit. The next Saturday, your new bunny is safe and sound in his new home. You name him Buster.

You do well the first few weeks, but after that we have to remind you every couple of days to feed and water Buster. Soon, we are doing it for you because you forget so often. One day, you come home from school and tell Mom you are just going to get a quick bite to eat before heading back to the school to play with some friends.

"Oh, no, you don't," Mom says. "Not today. You've got to clean Buster's cage, put new food in his container, clear out all the stuff from underneath him, and clip his nails. There's a big thunderstorm coming in and we're supposed to be getting rain for a few days. You go outside and take care of your pet."

Questions to Think On

- *Pets are fun to have, but a pain to feed and keep clean. If you had a pet, how would you do as its owner?*

- *Why do you think parents are so careful about getting a pet for their kids?*

- *If you failed to take care of your pet, how would you feel if we got rid of it?*

- *Mom and Dad: How can you tell if your child is ready to take care of a pet? Would you give it away if the pet wasn't properly cared for?*

What Does God Have to Say?

A righteous man cares for the needs of his animal, but the kindest acts of the wicked are cruel.   **Proverbs 12:10**

62 ■ Answering Tough Questions

What If...

One of the girls from your neighborhood started coming to church with you a couple of months ago. At first, she just came to the fun events: parties, hikes and so on. After she got to know a few of the other kids, she wasn't so shy. Even though her parents didn't go to church, she eventually started coming to Sunday school and church services with you.

She likes to go because it's something different to do on a Sunday. Her parents and older brother sleep in so there's never any conflict.

The past couple of weeks the teacher has been talking about what it means to be a Christian. He has used phrases such as "give your life to Christ," "start a relationship with God through Jesus Christ" and "turn your life over to the Lord." This has confused your friend. She thought that she was a Christian because she went to church. You tell her there's more to it than that.

She starts to ask you about what you believe:

- What do you think God is like?
- Why did Jesus have to die on a cross?
- Is he really the only way to get to God?
- Do you think I'm going to heaven?
- How do you start a "relationship with God"?

Questions to Think On

- *Take each of the questions above and answer them as best you can.* (Mom or Dad: If your child gets stuck and wants your help, try to answer them.)
- *If your friend says that she is ready to become a Christian, what would you say?*
- *Should you ask her to talk to her parents first?*
- *What if she doesn't want to become a Christian, but wants to keep coming to church?*

What Does God Have to Say?

I and the Father are one.   John 10:30

Jesus answered: "Don't you know me, Philip, even after I have been among you such a long time? Anyone who has seen me has seen the Father." **John 14:9**

63 ■ Here Am I, Send...

What If...

Saturdays usually provide you with a few good choices of things to do: relax, do chores, spend time with the family. Most of the time you end up doing all three. This week, you're faced with two different choices.

On Wednesday you get a call from the head of the deacon board. He says that since it's the holidays, there is an unusual number of families who need food. He asks if you'd mind delivering food to about a dozen homes from 10:00 A.M to 3:00 P.M. Checking your calendar, you see it's a clear day. "Sure, I'll be glad to do it."

Friday at work, the boss comes up and says that a couple of employees have had some health problems and he could sure use a hand on Saturday. He says he'll pay you time and a half for the day since it'll be overtime. He doesn't make it an order, but he knows you could use the money. He'd like you to do it because you're one of his best workers.

You tell him you'll check your calendar and see what you have scheduled. When you check, you remember that you agreed to deliver food baskets for the church.

You're in a real dilemma. You said you'd help out, but you know your boss wants you to work (and you *could* use the money).

Questions to Think On

- *What would you do?*
- *It's tempting to make a choice based on how it will benefit you. Why is this not always the best idea?*
- *How important to you is keeping your word?*
- *Has God ever "paid you back" for some bit of kindness you've done for others in his name?*

What Does God Have to Say?

Give, and it will be given to you. A good measure, pressed down, shaken together and running over, will be poured into your lap. For with the measure you use, it will be measured to you.   **Luke 6:38**

My conscience is clear, but that does not make me innocent. It is the Lord who judges me. Therefore judge nothing before the appointed time; wait till the Lord comes. He will bring to light what is hidden in darkness and will expose the motives of men's hearts. At that time each will receive his praise from God.   **1 Corinthians 4:4–5**

64 ■ Choose Wisely

What If...

Dad is in the military. That means our family has to move around a lot. About every three years Dad gets a new assignment and we have to sell our home and find another–usually in another state. That also means you have to make all new friends at a new school.

Just as you finish fifth grade, you find out you have to

move. The new school you'll be attending isn't a grade school, but a middle school. No more recess and lots more studying! Well, you take it in stride and try not to look too disappointed.

The first day of school you make friends with a couple of guys who play football at lunch time. You are a pretty good athlete, so you know that by getting involved in a game, you can meet some new guys. As usual, the athletic group at school seems to be popular. If you can be friends with a couple of the top athletes, you will be friends with all of their friends, too.

Not only are you an athlete, but you also play trombone in the school band. Though you aren't as good on the trombone as you are at sports, you like it all the same. The second day of class you get to know another trombone player. You really hit it off. He invites you over to his house and you find out you have quite a bit in common. That week, however, you discover a slight problem. This band guy has a reputation of being a nerd. He doesn't hang around with the athletes; they don't even know he exists.

As the weeks go by, you begin to notice that the athletes quit calling you. They even quit saying hi to you in the halls. The reason: you spend most of your lunch hours with your band friend. Now it looks like he is going to be your only friend.

Questions to Think On

- *What do you value most in a friend?*
- *Do you think once you hit junior high or middle school that popularity will be important?*
- *What would you do in this situation: go back to the popular group or stick with your one buddy?*

- *Mom and Dad: Did you ever have to make a choice about what group to hang out with?*

What Does God Have to Say?

A righteous man is cautious in friendship, but the way of the wicked leads them astray.   Proverbs 12:26

Fear of man will prove to be a snare, but whoever trusts in the Lord is kept safe.   Proverbs 29:25

65 ■ Light-Fingered Friends

What If...

It's Saturday afternoon and you're on your way to the store with a few friends from the neighborhood. You know them pretty well because you've been playing with them for years. They don't go to church, but for the most part, they're good friends.

When you hit the store you go straight to the ice cream section. You've got a $1.80 in your pocket and you think you'll have enough for a Dove Bar. Your friends fan out throughout the store in search of whatever goodies they want.

As you're standing in line two of them just go right through without buying anything. They motion for you to come with them, but you've got to pay for your ice cream. They motion again, but you point to the Dove Bar and wait your turn.

As you get to the front of the line, you see a third friend pass the registers without buying anything.

That's weird, you think. *Looks like I'm going to be the only one with something to eat. I suppose I'll have to share.*

When you get outside, everyone else is down by the corner of the store. Walking closer to them, you see they're munching away on candy bars.

"Where'd you get that stuff?" you ask.

"From the nice folks at the store, of course," one says. "We tried to get you out of there so you wouldn't have to waste your money, but you were clueless."

"Clueless about what? Did you steal that stuff?"

"Hey, with such poor security, they deserve to have stuff stolen from them. That was the easiest store I've ever stolen from."

You're having a tough time believing they actually stole that candy, but the truth of it is being stuffed into their faces.

"Here, take a Reese's," one of them says, offering you one of your favorite candy bars.

Questions to Think On

• *Knowing that was a stolen candy bar, what would you do or say?*

• *When are you most tempted to take something that doesn't belong to you?*

• *What do you think should be the consequences if you steal?*

• *Mom and Dad: When you were kids, did you ever steal anything? Did you get caught? What happened?*

What Does God Have to Say?

He who conceals his sins does not prosper, but whoever confesses and renounces them finds mercy.

Proverbs 28:13

Ill-gotten treasures are of no value, but righteousness delivers from death. **Proverbs 10:2**

66 ■ Speaking Up Is Hard to Do

What If...

It's discussion time again in science class. You are studying old civilizations and archaeology, how cultures developed from having no written language to having an advanced written language.

"Millions of years ago, well after human beings evolved from the sea," your teacher says, "they still communicated by a primitive form of language. As the human brain evolved into something much larger and complex, each tribe had those who would tell the history of their people on a continual basis. This is what is known as oral history."

"When did people start writing things down?" a student asks.

"That's a good question," the teacher says. "About 2500 B.C. some of the first writing occurred in Mesopotamia. Then later, the Jewish people began writing down their history as it had been handed down from past generations.

"So you see," she continues, "the evolution of man is still taking place. We have gone from being cave dwellers who drew pictures, to cultures that constructed and wrote down their own individual languages, to a computer-based society where we can process millions of commands a minute on a tiny microchip."

She used that word three times, you think. *I don't really believe in evolution. Should I say something?*

"Ah, Mrs. Williams," you say while raising your hand.

"Yes?"

"Isn't evolution just a theory? I mean, it can't really be proven. I believe that God had a reason for creating us and that we're not an accident."

"You must come from a churchgoing home," she says. "If

that's what your family wants to teach, that's fine. I'm sure there are others who believe the same. But science is pretty sure on this one. We're not going to talk about creation because there is even less proof for that theory. And because it's a church-related matter, we really can't talk about it at all, so I'd appreciate it if you didn't bring it up again."

Later at recess, a couple of kids say they were glad you raised your hand and spoke up. But then you also hear a few people call you "the churchmeister."

Questions to Think On

- *You may not have faced a situation like this but you might if you're in a public school. What do you think you would say if evolution was taught as fact?*
- *By speaking up, you let others know that you're a Christian. How do you feel about that?*
- *Would people really care that much if they knew you went to church?*
- *Mom and Dad: What are some things your child can say when this issue comes up in school?*

What Does God Have to Say?

Blessed are you when people insult you, persecute you and falsely say all kinds of evil against you because of me. Rejoice and be glad, because great is your reward in heaven, for in the same way they persecuted the prophets who were before you.   Matthew 5:11–12

You are the light of the world. A city on a hill cannot be hidden. Neither do people light a lamp and put it under a bowl. Instead they put it on its stand, and it gives light to everyone in the house. In the same way, let your light shine before men, that they may see your good deeds and praise your Father in heaven.   **Matthew 5:14-16**

67 ▪ The Chatterbox

What If...

You're very social; you have *lots* of friends. And because you have so many friends, you feel like you need to talk to them more often than just at school. That means you're on the phone quite a bit, catching up with everyone on how they're doing with their homework, how they're getting along with their brothers and sisters, new things they've heard, stuff like that.

You are known to talk on the phone for up to four hours on weekends. Needless to say, Mom and Dad aren't happy to have you tie up the family phone for so long. Your solution seems logical–get your own phone and number for your room–but we don't think that's a good idea.

Finally, we have had enough.

"We need to talk about your phone use," Dad tells you one evening. "You've been on the phone almost nonstop since I got home from work. It's got to end. From now on, you are limited to thirty minutes a day on the phone."

"Thirty minutes! Dad, that's not enough. I've got to talk more than that."

"Sorry. We've let you get away with too much for too long. No more. You've got to get this phone thing under control, and we're going to help."

Well, you do your best to keep to the time limit, but

pretty soon you're sneaking the cordless phone to the bathroom, and doing everything you can to keep in touch with your friends.

As can be expected, Mom catches you and tells Dad. The consequences: a week with no phone privileges.

That makes you mad, but not as mad as two weeks later, when Dad catches you using the phone more than allowed. He gives you a one-month suspension!

Questions to Think On

- *When we discipline you, do you think we want to or have to?*
- *If we never disciplined you for deliberate disobedience, how do you think you'd turn out?*
- *Do we ever seem unfair in our punishment? In what ways?*
- *Would you rather we just punish you, or give you a choice as to what "medicine" you need to take?*

What Does God Have to Say?

He who spares the rod hates his son, but he who loves him is careful to discipline him.   **Proverbs 13:24**

He who ignores discipline despises himself, but whoever heeds correction gains understanding.   **Proverbs 15:32**

My son, do not despise the Lord's discipline and do not resent his rebuke, because the Lord disciplines those he loves, as a father the son he delights in.   **Proverbs 3:11–12**

68 ▪ The Big Letdown

What If...

Your son has been playing basketball out in the driveway for years. You go out and rebound for him when you have time. Once in a while, you give him a few pointers on how to dribble and shoot a lay-up. As he's grown, you've gone to his games all through his grade school years–almost every one!

As he improves his play, you are always there to give him encouragement. And then there are those games of "horse" he ropes you into. You try all of the trick shots you know; make a few, too. When he complains, you shoot something normal. He's at the point where he can beat you on a consistent basis. Win or lose, you always have a way of making it close so he doesn't get too discouraged.

Now it's basketball season again and your son is in his first year of junior high school. He's never had any trouble making a team before, so you don't even think about him not making this one.

He comes home from practice one day with a worried look on his face. At dinner he says, "The competition is pretty tough this year. There are quite a few new guys who are a lot better than me. I don't know if I'll make the team."

This confession catches everyone by surprise. You tell him to try his best, "that's all you can do."

Three days later, he comes home right after school. You got home early, and you're surprised to see him walk in the door. As he heads down the hallway you can see he's been crying.

"Why aren't you at practice?" you ask.

He hesitates a little as he goes into his room. "I got cut," is all he says as he closes the door.

Questions to Think On

- *What would you do or say to try to comfort him?*
- *Have you ever been so disappointed about something that happened to you that no words could help you feel better?*
- *When you feel that way, what is the best way others can encourage you?*
- *Are you a good encourager? Do you like to build others up by what you say?*

What Does God Have to Say

A man finds joy in giving an apt reply–and how good is a timely word.   Proverbs 15:23

A cheerful look brings joy to the heart, and good news gives health to the bones.   Proverbs 15:30

69 ■ The Tough Guy

What If...

Since you were in kindergarten, soccer has been your sport. You haven't missed a season, spring or fall. Playing competitively, you know soccer as well as anyone your age. You know the positions, the penalties, how to hit the far post goal; you know the game.

You also know how to play in a controlled, aggressive way. That is, most of the time the contact you initiate is legal and fair.

At a tournament in another town, you play against a team you've never played before. As a right-winger, your job is to be one of the first players to push up when the ball crosses midfield. The player who is marking you is a little bigger than you—and rough. On a couple of plays early in the game he puts a hard check on you to steal the ball and move it the other way. You look at the ref for a call, but it never comes. At halftime, the score is still tied at zero.

The second half begins and you take the ball down the side. The same player moves up on you and rams you right to the ground. Finally, the whistle blows. The ref pulls out his yellow card and raises it in the air.

That will keep him off of me for a while, you think. *He's got to back off and play fair now.* And he does… for about another ten minutes. That's when your team scores. In this game, with your defense playing so well, that goal could be the game winner.

Now the defense controls the ball and switches it to your side of the field. As you race down the sideline, you see that same player coming for you again, so you stop the ball and dribble it to the middle. This catches him off guard, but he quickly recovers and starts for you again—this time from behind. Just as you enter the goal box, he puts a hard trip on you from behind. Quickly the ref blows his whistle, calls the other player over and gives him a red card! Not only is he out of the game, but this eliminates him from the next game in the tournament, too.

The coach lets you shoot the penalty shot and you put it in. The games ends, you've won two to nothing.

After the game it's customary for the teams to line up and shake hands at the center of the field. As the other player passes by you have to decide what you'll say or do.

Questions to Think On
• *What would you feel like doing?*

- *What do you think the word "gloat" means?*
- *When you beat someone, whether it's in a sport or a game, do you like to rub it in?*
- *Mom and Dad: What do you think is the correct way to win gracefully?*

What Does God Have to Say?

You should not look down on your brother in the day of his misfortune, nor rejoice over the people of Judah in the day of their destruction, nor boast so much in the day of their trouble.   **Obadiah 12**

But when I stumbled, they gathered in glee; attackers gathered against me when I was unaware. The slandered me without ceasing.   **Psalm 35:15**

70 ■ The Fruit of Your Labors

What If...

You're not known for being smart. Oh, your report cards aren't ever bad and you participate in class discussions a lot, but you're not known as The Brain. The best you've ever done is two A's and the rest B's.

However, this year you decide to try your absolute hardest to see how high you can get your grades. All of the studying cuts into your play and TV time a little, but you're determined to do your best.

Your midway grades look good. Four A's and only two B's. Mom and Dad are impressed. So is your teacher. He comments about it the next day at school. That makes you even more determined. You really believe it's possible to get straight As for the quarter.

Every day after school, the first thing you do is your homework. If you don't understand something, you ask Mom (who seems to always know the answer and points you in the right direction).

On the final day of the quarter you get your grades. Opening the envelope you see they are all A's!! Immediately, you start asking everyone around how they did on their grades–so they will ask you how you did. If they don't ask, you tell them anyway.

"I got straight A's!" you say, waiting for them to say something nice to you. After you work your way through nearly the whole class, your teacher sees what's happening. He comes over and says he's glad you did so well, but you shouldn't be bragging so much; most of the kids didn't do as well as you.

Questions to Think On

- *What does the word "brag" mean to you?*
- *It's natural to want others to notice you when you do well in something, but some people overdo it. How do you feel when others brag about something they've done?*
- *Do you feel like you get enough attention at home for the good things you do?*
- *What would you rather have someone do: notice you after you mention something good you've done, or notice you before you tell about what you did?*

What Does God Have to Say?

Do you see a man wise in his own eyes? There is more hope for a fool than for him.   **Proverbs 26:12**

Likewise the tongue is a small part of the body, but it makes great boasts. Consider what a great forest is set on fire by a small spark.   **James 3:5**

71 ■ What a Chore!

What If...

You like this family a lot. You like our home, our neighborhood, our church, even your school. The one thing you're not that crazy about, though, is chores. Those little jobs that always seem to get in the way of your fun... at the exact moment that it's the funnest!

Every week it's the same thing: clean your room, take out the upstairs trash, empty the dishwasher, fold the clothes. Yes, you get your allowance for doing all of those little things, but sometimes you'd almost rather not get anything. The reason? Mom and Dad constantly have to remind you to do them. We threaten to take away that allowance, not let you watch TV, not let you play with your friends–we try anything that involves withholding privileges.

You try to be logical about the situation. *Why should I do chores?* you think. *I'm a kid. Kids are supposed to have fun, not work.*

And you are a typical kid. You like to play in your room with some of your special games and collections, you like to watch TV when there's something good on (even when there isn't sometimes), you love to spend time with your friends... you love to do anything and everything–besides work.

Lately, it's been a real source of "discussion" between

Mom and Dad and you. We can't convince you to do your chores, and you can't convince us why you shouldn't do them.

Questions to Think On

- *Though it may not be this serious at our house when it comes to chores, think about it from Mom and Dad's side for a minute: why do we really want you to do chores?*
- *Do you think it's fair for us to do all of the work?*
- *What do you think the word "responsibility" means?*
- *Mom and Dad: Explain your reasoning behind giving your child the chores you do.*

What Does God Have to Say?

He who works his land will have abundant food, but he who chases fantasies lacks judgment.   **Proverbs 12:11**

Remind the people to be subject to rulers and authorities, to be obedient, to be ready to do whatever is good.

Titus 3:1

72 ■ The Captain's Tough Choice

What If...

It's lunch recess again, so it's time for everyone to line up to be selected for the softball game. The routine is always the same: everyone lines up while the two captains pick their teams. Since you're a pretty good athlete, you're always one of the first few to get picked. No one ever seems to complain, but you've wondered how Cheri feels. She's always picked last.

One day, the kids who usually pick teams aren't around so you're told to go out and pick. You've never had this chance before. Suddenly, you know how it feels to be a captain. You want to have good players so you can beat the other team.

Your first two picks are your best friends, while the other captain picks two good players. You can see where this is leading. Cheri is going to be picked last again unless you break with tradition. You could surprise everyone by picking her third, but then you'd be stuck with someone who can't throw the ball and can barely catch.

Questions to Think On

- *What would you do?*
- *How do you think it would make Cheri feel if she wasn't picked last for once? How would you feel if it were you who was always picked last?*
- *How important is it for you to win? Does anyone really care who wins and loses?*
- *Though you probably know what Jesus would do, why is it so hard to do that?*

What Does God Have to Say?

Therefore, as God's chosen people, holy and dearly loved, clothe yourselves with compassion, kindness, humility, gentleness and patience.   **Colossians 3:12**

Each of you should look not only to your own interests, but also to the interests of others.   **Philippians 2:4**

73 ■ Leave It Where You Put It

What If...

Mom, you receive a phone call from your dad right at the end of the dinner hour. Dad and we kids notice that you're quiet for the first few minutes. Then you start asking questions in a low, broken voice. We can't hear them all, and we know you're trying not to cry.

When you hang up the phone you tell the family that Grandpa says Grandma has cancer. Then you really start crying.

Dad, you immediately go and hug her, then suggest that we go into the living room to pray. We all get down on our knees and take turns praying. Mom prays, too, though it's hard for her to get her words out.

As the days go by there are more phone calls and visits, but each night the family prays together. In the mornings, Dad, you and Mom pray while we're still in bed. Both of you realize that Grandma is in God's hands. She has always had a strong faith, and besides the little bit of pain and discomfort she's in, her spirits are pretty good. Grandpa's holding up as best he can.

But Mom, you are having a hard time. As the weeks go by, you sound frustrated in your prayers and it almost seems like you don't really believe God is doing his job of handling the situation. When you pray you give Grandma over to God, but throughout the rest of the day you seem to take her back and worry about her all over again.

Questions to Think On

- *Hopefully this situation will never happen to our family. But praying, then "taking back the situation" and worrying about it is com-*

mon (or so says the writer of this book). Have either you or Dad ever done this before?

- How does taking back a problem that you've given to God help or hurt you?
- What types of things are easy for you and Dad to pray about and leave in God's hands? What are the toughest?
- Has God ever proven to be untrustworthy when you've given him something to take care of?

What Does God Have to Say?

Therefore I tell you, whatever you ask for in prayer, believe that you have received it, and it will be yours.

Mark 11:24

I cry out to God Most High, to God, who fulfills his purpose for me. He sends from heaven and saves me, rebuking those who hotly pursue me; God sends his love and his faithfulness.

Psalm 57:2-3

74 ■ He Still Does Miracles

What If...

You wake up one morning not feeling good at all. You're feverish, but even with all of the covers on, you still feel chilled. When we come into your room to get you up for school, we see you don't look so hot. You're not faking anything to stay home... you're sick with the flu!

Staying home from school is normally pretty fun, but when you're this sick, all you can do is lie in bed or on the couch and wait for it to go away. You have absolutely no energy to do anything that requires even the least amount of effort.

Before Dad leaves for work, he and Mom come into your room to pray for you. He prays that God will heal you this morning, and that you won't be sick all day long. Mom prays the same thing. We seem so confident, as if God can really heal a flu in a few hours when it usually takes a day to work its way through your system.

About nine o'clock that morning, the chills stop and your head isn't as warm as it was when you woke up. A half hour later you notice that you're hungry, so you walk out to the kitchen to tell Mom. She feels your head, then takes your temperature. It's 98.8! Almost normal!

After eating breakfast you still feel great and head off to your room to play. Then it hits you: Mom and Dad both prayed that you'd get well this morning. God answered our prayers!

Questions to Think On

- *Have you ever seen God answer a prayer in such an immediate, obvious way like this before?*

- *How do you respond when you notice that God has answered your prayers?*

- *Though God doesn't answer every one of our prayers so quickly, sometimes he does. Is God still answering your prayers when he chooses to take a little longer to do it?*

- *Mom and Dad: Talk about times when it has been obvious that God has answered your prayers in a miraculous way.*

What Does God Have to Say?

Ask and it will be given to you; seek and you will find; knock and the door will be opened to you. For everyone who asks receives; he who seeks finds; and to him who knocks, the door will be opened.   Matthew 7:7-8

I urge, then, first of all, that requests, prayers, intercession and thanksgiving be made for everyone.   1 Timothy 2:1

75 ■ The "One Up" Game

What If...

You are with your friends and this conversation takes place:

"Hey, where'd you get that bike, the Salvation Army kiddie store?" one friend asks you.

"As a matter of fact, no. My parents got it for me at Olympic Bikes," you say. "But Jones over there told me you were hoping to get some Barney underwear for Christmas. I'll be sure to tell your parents for you."

"Hey, guys, cool off," says Jones. "After all, when you start putting each other down, you look and sound like idiots. Can't we just have a normal conversation once in a while?"

"Thanks for the idiot lesson, Jones. I guess it takes one to know one."

"Speaking of lessons," you say. "Did you hear that Abbott was taking violin lessons? Can you imagine anyone playing the violin?"

"Now why would you rank on a guy for taking violin?" Jones asks. "Who made you the decider of what people should do? If you had your way, you'd want everyone to play football or something."

"At least I *can* play football, Mr. Wimp," you retort.

And on it goes for another five minutes, each of you

trying to outdo the other, sarcastically putting each other down. It's like that a lot with your friends. Some are good at it, others aren't.

Questions to Think On
- *How can sarcastic humor be hurtful?*
- *Have someone else's jokes about you ever hurt your feelings? What did you do about it?*
- *When you put someone else down, what are you really trying to do?*
- *Mom and Dad: What are the rules around the house about sarcastic humor and put-downs? Why?*

What Does God Have to Say?
A man who lacks judgment derides his neighbor, but a man of understanding holds his tongue.   **Proverbs 11:12**

The righteous will never be uprooted, but the wicked will not remain in the land. The mouth of the righteous brings forth wisdom, but a perverse tongue will be cut out.
                                        Proverbs 10:30–31

76 ■ Where Freedom Can Lead

What If...
You're home alone on a Saturday afternoon. We have taken your brother to a birthday party and then are going to do a little shopping. We said we wouldn't be gone long.

Since you rarely get the chance to be alone in the middle of the day, you feel like you should take advantage of the freedom. So you go into the kitchen to get a soda and some chips, then head down to the living room to watch some TV. About an hour later, you're back up to the kitchen again to get some ice cream. A while later, it's peanuts and lemonade.

When we get home you tell us what you've been doing. About a half hour later, Mom asks you what you want for dinner.

"Can we order out for pizza and eat it downstairs in front of the TV?" you ask.

"Well, we haven't done that in a while," she replies. "I suppose."

After pizza and more soda–and another two hours of TV–you ask for some Cocoa Krispies before going to bed.

Sunday morning comes and you wake up at about 7:00. You're not feeling so hot. Your stomach is doing some major aerobic exercises.

"Mom, Dad, I'm not feeling so hot. Can I stay home from church?"

"What's the problem?" Dad asks.

"My stomach doesn't feel too good. I think I'd just like to lie down in front of the TV."

Questions to Think On

- *While this may be an extreme example, it's tempting to use your freedom to overload on a good thing. Have you ever done something like this before?*

- *What are you most tempted to overdo: TV, junk food, video games, sports, music or something else?*

- *When we overdo on one thing, that usually means something else has to give. Often it's reading our Bibles or praying. Do you think Satan wants to distract you from following Christ? How is he doing that in your life right now?*

- *Mom and Dad: How do you know when to stop or slow down when a good thing is getting to be too much?*

What Does God Have to Say?

If you find honey, eat just enough–too much of it, and you will vomit.   **Proverbs 25:16**

But I am afraid that just as Eve was deceived by the serpent's cunning, your minds may somehow be led astray from your sincere and pure devotion to Christ.

2 Corinthians 11:3

77 ■ When Believing Isn't Seeing

What If...

The topic of faith in Jesus Christ doesn't come up too much with you and your friends. Occasionally, belief in God will be mentioned–and a few of your friends *do* go to church. The ones who don't go know that you're a regular attender. One thing's for sure: most of them don't really understand what it means to be a Christian.

At soccer practice one day, the coach lets everyone know that the tournament game will be Sunday at 10:30 A.M. and that you need to be there forty-five minutes before game time.

One kid speaks up, "Coach, I'm not sure I can go. We have church on Sundays, and my parents don't like to miss it."

The coach looks at his assistant and rolls his eyes.

"Well, I understand," he says. "You ask your parents if you could just miss this Sunday, then call me tonight."

"OK."

"Does anyone else have a conflict?" the coach asks.

You raise your hand. "I might miss it too because of church, Coach."

Again, he gives his assistant a frustrated look.

As you're gathering your stuff together, a few teammates try to convince you and the other player to skip church. They're being friendly about it, but you know they don't understand. Just then the assistant coach tries to get in on the conversation.

"I never had this problem when I was playing club soccer," he says. "My parents told me never to believe anything I couldn't see. They said trust your eyes and your instincts, not some invisible God who may not be there. You ought to consider that same advice."

Questions to Think On

- *What the coach says sounds logical, but there are many things we believe in that we can't see. Can you name a few? (wind, people in history, electricity)*
- *Do other classmates ever challenge you on your beliefs? In what ways?*
- *Why do you think God doesn't reveal himself to people if he wants them to believe in him? (Mom or Dad, give your answer.)*
- *Is it easy or hard for you to believe in someone you can't see?*

What Does God Have to Say?

And without faith it is impossible to please God, because anyone who comes to him must believe that he exists and that he rewards those who earnestly seek him.

Hebrews 11:6

Now faith is being sure of what we hope for and certain of what we do not see. **Hebrews 11:1**

78 ■ "The Least of These..."

What If...

You are walking downtown with our family on a Saturday morning. There is a farmer's market street sale every weekend where fruit and vegetables and other types of good food are sold. We go to it two or three times a year.

It is approaching fall and the weather isn't all that warm. After we walk through the market a couple of times, we all decide to go to the pioneer museum a short distance away. On our way there we pass a park where some people dressed in old clothes are just hanging out. Some are seated, a few are lying down on the park benches. They look asleep.

"Who are those people?" I ask you.

"Those people are probably the homeless," you say. "Each day they come here to be in the sun. When it gets dark they go some place where they can sleep and stay warm–a shelter or mission or something."

After taking our tour through the museum, we head back to our car. Walking by the park again, we see a mom sitting on the grass with two of her kids. The kids are crawling around and the mom is just staring into space.

Questions to Think On

- *Can you think of anything to do for this mom and her kids?*
- *What do you think a Christian should do to help the poor and homeless?*

- *Have you ever thought about doing something for these people as a family?*
- *Why don't we try to do more to help these people?*

What Does God Have to Say?

A generous man will prosper; he who refreshes others will himself be refreshed.   **Proverbs 11:25**

He who gives to the poor will lack nothing, but he who closes his eyes to them receives many curses.
                                                                    Proverbs 28:27

Rich and poor have this in common: The Lord is the Maker of them all.   **Proverbs 22:2**

79 ■ Rebuffed?

What If...

Every school year you have to get used to a new teacher. You also have to:

- Do more homework.
- Worry about looking good in your class pictures.
- Get to know a few more kids in your class that weren't there last year.

OK, so it's not major stuff, but that last one often causes the most excitement... and stress.

But what if you were the new kid in town? Imagine heading into a big school of hundreds of different faces and a classroom with at least thirty other strangers. You'd feel out of place, lonely.

This school year there are five new faces in your class. Each has moved in from another part of the state. Instead of letting time take care of their jitters and fear (which it will), you decide to try to make friends with one of them before class even starts.

"Hi, my name's Lynn. What's yours?" you say.

"Hi, I'm Terry. When does class start?"

The bell rings.

"Right now. I'll see you at recess."

No response.

When it's time for recess, you look for Terry right away.

"Hey, do you want to go play on the monkey bars?" you ask.

"No, I don't think so."

"How about basketball?"

"No. Do you know where the teacher goes? I gotta ask her something."

"She's over there," you say, pointing toward the building.

Terry runs over to her without saying another word.

Questions to Think On

- *If this happened to you, what would you be thinking about how much Terry wants to hang around with you?*

- *Are you the type who would be persistent or would you take Terry's remarks as a sign that she doesn't want to spend time with you?*

- *Are you the type who jumps to hasty conclusions about people and situations or do you usually give things more time?*

- *What do you think are the consequences for being hasty in your opinions and decisions?*

What Does God Have to Say?

It is not good to have zeal without knowledge, nor to be hasty and miss the way.   Proverbs 19:2

Do you see a man who speaks in haste? There is more hope for a fool than for him.   **Proverbs 29:20**

80 ■ Friday Night Fights

What If...

It's Friday night and your favorite TV shows are on. You've been waiting all week to see them. When your brother comes in, though, it's a different story.

"We're not going to watch those shows again this week," he says. "I'm sick of them and it's my week to watch what I want."

"No way, we always watch these shows on Friday night."

"Forget it. I asked Mom and Dad and they said I could watch what I wanted tonight."

"No, they didn't, you're lying. Where are they?"

"They went for a walk and won't be back for probably a half hour."

"Well, you can't change the channel until they're back."

"Oh yeah, watch me," he says as he gets up and changes the channel.

"Cut it out!" you yell as you jump up to change it back.

"Make me," he says.

And with that statement, you rear back and give him a hard push. He falls backwards and hits his head on the coffee table.

"There, are you satisfied?" you say while changing the station.

He takes his hand off of his aching head and looks at it. You can see blood on it. He's cut his head. Now you're in for it. There's evidence of a fight.

When we get back from our walk, he tells us the whole story.

Questions to Think On
- *What would you try to say to defend yourself?*
- *Should you be punished for what you did? How much?*
- *Would you feel like apologizing? How good are you at saying you're sorry when you've done something wrong?*
- *Mom and Dad: What would the consequences be for this type of behavior?*

What Does God Have to Say?

Repent, then, and turn to God, so that your sins may be wiped out, that times of refreshing may come from the Lord, and that he may send the Christ, who has been appointed for you–even Jesus.   **Acts 3:19–20**

Produce fruit in keeping with repentance.   **Matthew 3:8**

81 ■ Taking the After–School Challenge

What If...

It's Tuesday night and you're kicking back, watching TV. The phone rings, and you jump to answer it. It's a friend from class! She wants to know if you can come over to her house after school tomorrow. Laying the phone receiver down, you race upstairs to Mom. She's says it's fine as long as your friend's mom is home. You go back to the phone and ask if her mom works. When she says no, you say you can come and stay until about five.

The next day, you see your friend and confirm plans to walk home together. Everything is set, but something's weird. She asks if you like to try new things.

"Well, sometimes. It depends on what it is," you say.

"I'm not going to tell you, but it's really cool. You'll like it," she says.

As she walks away, she turns around and laughs.

I wonder what she's got on her mind, you think.

After school, you walk the half mile to her house. She doesn't bring it up again, so you're feeling better about going over. You talk about the day, your homework, and what you're going to do on the weekend.

As you walk up her driveway, she says you need to head around back to get in.

"Why?" you ask.

"Because my mom's not home, so we have to get in through the sliding glass door," she says.

"I thought you said your mom didn't work?"

"She doesn't. She's helping my grandma do some shopping today and won't be home 'til about 4:30. She trusts me, I guess. My older brother will be home from high school at about 4:00.

"Hey, remember at recess today when I asked you if you liked to try new things?" she asks.

"Yeah."

"Well, have you ever tried smoking cigarettes?"

"What? Are you kidding? Why would I want to do that?"

"'Cause it's cool. Come on, I'll grab a couple of my dad's and we'll go out in the backyard by that big tree. No one will know."

"I don't know," you say. "What if we get caught?"

"We're not going to get caught, believe me. I'm not going to tell anyone, are you?"

"Well... no. But your mom was supposed to be home, and if my mom finds out she wasn't, she'll be pretty mad. I think I'd better call her."

"You're chicken, aren't you?"

Questions to Think On

- *What would you say if she said that?*

- *Besides cigarettes, what else could a friend offer that would be a bad idea to take?*

- *What would have been the best plan once you found out her parents weren't home?*

- *Mom and Dad: Did you ever try something like this when you were a kid? What happened?*

What Does God Have to Say?

Do not join those who drink too much wine or gorge themselves on meat, for drunkards and gluttons become poor, and drowsiness clothes them in rags.

Proverbs 23:20-21

Who has woe? Who has sorrow? Who has strife? Who has complaints? Who has needless bruises? Who has bloodshot eyes? Those who linger over wine, who go to sample bowls of mixed wine.   Proverbs 23:29-30

82 ■ Only One Way?

What If...

Having the relatives over for Christmas Day is always... interesting. Mom's family members aren't Christians, so your cousins don't always say or do things that are normal for your home. Oh, they're not bad kids, but every once in awhile they will cut loose with a swear word, and they don't even think about praying before a meal... and their music, especially your older cousin Jeff's—let's just say it doesn't come close to resembling what you listen to.

With new toys and games around, though, there's usually enough to keep everyone busy for the day.

After the midafternoon meal, while the dads are cleaning up the kitchen and the moms are watching TV (*yeah, right*), you head outside to ride bikes with your cousin. As you're going down the street, she asks you a question.

"Why do you guys always pray before meals?"

Though it catches you off guard, you know the answer to that one. "Because we believe in God and go to church, I guess."

"When I was little, we used to go every Sunday, but we quit a long time ago. Why would you want to go? I mean, it's boring, isn't it? Remember last year when we went to Christmas Eve service with you guys?"

"Yeah."

"Well, that's why we came on Christmas Day this year; so we wouldn't have to go again. I fell asleep."

"I know your family doesn't believe in God or Jesus," you say, "but we do. We think Christmas is a special time of year."

"Our family believes in God, and my dad says Jesus Christ a lot, but we don't think you need to go to church to get to heaven."

Questions to Think On

- *What would you say next? Do you have to go to church to get to heaven?*

- *Since your cousin probably just believes what her parents believe, what are ways you could get her thinking about Jesus Christ in a more positive way? (Mom or Dad, you can help if need be.)*

- *What are different roads people think they can go down to get to heaven? (talk about the church road, the good works road, the giving money road, etc.)*

- *Mom and Dad: How would you answer questions from friends, neighbors, relatives and co-workers about why going through Jesus Christ to get to God is the only way to heaven?*

What Does God Have to Say?

My brothers, if one of you should wander from the truth and someone should bring him back, remember this: Whoever turns a sinner away from his error will save him from death and cover over a multitude of sins.

James 5:19–20

Salvation is found in no one else, for there is no other name under heaven given to men by which we must be saved. Acts 4:12

83 ■ The Whole Truth and Nothing But...

What If...

We've lived in our house for a number of years... but now it's time to move. Dad, you got a different job in another town, so we are going to have sell this house and find a new one.

We have a few months before we have to move and we need every bit of it to get the house fixed up. We do lots of yard work, paint a few rooms and generally work our tails off to get the house ready to sell.

Instead of using a real estate agent to help sell the house, you decide to market it on your own. You go to the local library and find books on how to do it. Then you go to an office supply store to get all of the necessary paperwork. Finally, you place an ad in the newspaper, put up a few signs and wait for offers.

A number of buyers come by; most have a lot of questions.

"That roof looks in bad shape. How old is it?" asks one.

"Well, not very old," you say (not really knowing the answer).

"Have you had any problems lately with the furnace?" asks another.

"Furnace? Lately? Well, you know, it's been running great for a long time," you say (knowing that it *has* acted up at times, but never too badly).

Other potential buyers come by with lots of questions about the foundation, water drainage, radon, heating and water bills—more questions than you thought were legal to ask!

You want to sell the house–and you need to sell it for a lot of money. If these people hear the real answers to the questions they are asking, they may not pay top dollar for the house.

Questions to Think On
- *What is the difference between a half-truth and a lie?*
- *In order to get a lot more money for the house, would you be tempted to not tell the whole truth?*
- *Whose responsibility is it to sell the house for the best price?*
- *What does the word integrity mean to you?*

What Does God Have to Say?
The man of integrity walks securely, but he who takes crooked paths will be found out.   **Proverbs 10:9**

He whose walk is blameless is kept safe, but he whose ways are perverse will suddenly fall.   **Proverbs 28:18**

84 ■ How Much Does Friendliness Cost?

What If...
As one of the more social kids at school, you have lots of friends. Nearly every week someone calls and asks you to come over to play. You, of course, love to go. Basketball, soccer, baseball, army, sports cards–whatever your friends want to do, you'll join in.

Naturally, you have four or five who are closer friends

than all the rest. These are kids you'll spend the night with, or who will spend the night with you. Then there are your friends at church. They are not quite as close because you don't spend as much time with them, but they're good guys.

One day while climbing the monkey bars at recess, a kid comes over to where you and your friend are showing off to the girls. He tries to join in. Now this guy is not one of your close friends. In fact, you've hardly even talked to him since school started. He hasn't learned how to fit in, he doesn't talk too much and isn't into sports (he's usually the last guy picked for football at lunchtime recess).

He's nice, but sometimes he tries a little too hard. While everyone is goofing off, he asks you if you can come over to his house after school the next day. All of your friends look at you, then him, then back at you.

Thinking quickly, you say you'll check with your mom and tell him tomorrow. You can almost predict that if you *do* go over to his house, it'll be boring because you don't have a lot in common. Plus, you're not sure you want him to start thinking of you as one of his friends.

Mom gives the predictable, "Fine with me."

Now you're faced with a dilemma: go over to the guy's house or somehow (without lying) let him know you don't want to.

Questions to Think On

- *What would you do and why?*
- *Are most loners weird, or have they just never been given a chance?*
- *What would be the disadvantages of going? How about the advantages?*
- *There are several reasons why some kids don't have many friends:*

they've moved a lot, their parents never taught them how to talk to others, they fear rejection (based on past experience). What can be done to bring someone up to a level where they can form friendships of their own?

What Does God Have to Say?

For the Son of Man came to seek and to save what was lost.   Luke 19:10

Greater love has no one than this, that he lay down his life for his friends.   John 15:13

85 ■ What to Do When You're Ready for More

What If...

You've been getting a two-dollars-a-week allowance for a couple of years now. All you have to do is keep your room clean, take out the garbage throughout the house the day before trash day, put the dishes away every other time and fold clothes when Mom asks. Now you are ready to move up.

"Dad, can I have a bigger allowance?" you ask one day out of the blue.

"Why?" Dad asks.

"Because I'm older now and I need more money."

"That's not a very good reason. But maybe we could think of a few more chores so I could pay you three dollars a week."

"Like what?"

"Well, how about if you set and clear the table every night?"

"I could do that. It's a deal!"

The first week of this new arrangement, you do fine. When Sunday comes, you collect your three dollars. The next week you start well, but by the end of it you only set and clear when you're reminded a couple of times. Dad reluctantly gives you your allowance.

By the third week, you let Mom set the table a couple of times, and run from the table early a few more times to watch the TV. When it comes time to collect your allowance, Dad only gives you two dollars.

"What's this?" you ask. "I thought we had a deal."

"We did, and you broke it. I'm sorry."

The following week you're thinking about wanting to get a stereo for your room, but you know that at two dollars a week, it'll take a year to get it.

"Mom, Dad," you say, "I've decided I'd like to get a paper route to help me make more money. Is that all right?"

Questions to Think On

- *What do you think we would say?*
- *Have you proven you can be faithful and responsible in smaller things in order to handle something as big as a paper route?*
- *Do you understand why we say no to some bigger privileges if you haven't done what you should with small responsibilities?*
- *Mom and Dad: Talk about the relationship between being faithful in small things in order to be trusted with larger privileges.*

What Does God Have to Say?

Again, it will be like a man going on a journey, who called his servants and entrusted his property to them. To one he gave five talents of money, to another two talents, and to another one talent, each according to his ability. Then he went on his journey. The man who had received the five talents went at once and put his money to work and gained five more. So also, the one with the two talents gained two more. But the man who had received the one talent went off, dug a hole in the ground and hid his master's money.

After a long time the master of those servants returned and settled accounts with them. The man who had received the five talents brought the other five. "Master," he said, "you entrusted me with five talents. See, I have gained five more."

His master replied, "Well done, good and faithful servant! You have been faithful with a few things; I will put you in charge of many things. Come and share your master's happiness!"   Matthew 25:14-21

86 ■ It's Not if You Win or Lose, It's...

What If...

Sunday school has its good points and bad points. One of the good things, though, is the Bible challenge game at the end of every class. It's usually girls versus guys, so that makes it even better. The reason: the girls nearly always win.

One particular Sunday, the competition is fierce. The guys have lost for two straight weeks and they are down again, five to three. The teacher plays moderator for the game, so he has the power to decide who raised their hand first—and therefore, who gets to answer the question.

He asks a question, and it looks to you like your team

has a hand up first. Instead, he says the guys' hands were up. They answer correctly, and it's five to four. The next question the same thing happens. Now it's tied, five to five. A few of the girls say that the teacher is giving the guys a break. He just smiles.

A few minutes later it's nine to nine. The next point wins. He asks the question and clearly the girls have their hands up first. The teacher calls on the guys and they answer correctly to win the game.

All of the girls complain in protest, and again, the teacher just smiles. Then he says, "Better luck next week."

This really ticks you off. It is obvious he was letting the guys win.

Questions to Think On

- *What would you do or say if this happened to you?*
- *What do you have the power to control: the way the leader plays the game, or your response to how he leads?*
- *What do you think is the right thing to do when you or your team is being treated unfairly (in any game or situation)?*
- *Have you ever treated someone unfairly? How does it make people feel?*

What Does God Have to Say?

Proverbs... for attaining wisdom and discipline; for understanding words of insight; for acquiring a disciplined and prudent life, doing what is right and just and fair.

Proverbs 1:2-3

He who walks righteously and speaks what is right, who rejects gain from extortion and keeps his hand from accepting bribes, who stops his ears against plots of murder and shuts his eyes against contemplating evil–this is the man who will dwell on the heights, whose refuge will be the mountain fortress. His bread will be supplied, and water will not fail him.   **Isaiah 33:15–16**

87 ■ It Doesn't Get Much Worse Than This

What If...

For the most part, your life has gone pretty well. You've got a family that loves you, a home that's comfortable, a good church, a bike, some friends, your own bed... hey, life *is* pretty good.

But then one week everything starts to go wrong.

You walk to school and accidentally drop your backpack in a huge mud puddle. Not only is the pack soggy, but all of your books, a class project that took you three weeks to work on and the rest of your homework is wet beyond recognition. Your books are so far gone that Mom and Dad have to buy new ones.

When you get home from school, you see that your stereo is gone. What happened? Your little sister was playing in your room and dropped it... twice. It was completely ruined so Mom threw it away.

The next day you ride your bike to school, but in your hurry to get to class you forget to lock it. When you head out the door to go home after school... you guessed it, someone stole your bike. The weather for the one-mile *walk* home? It's raining buckets, of course.

That night your dog gets really sick. He's making *bad*

messes all over the house. About bedtime, Dad decides you and he need to take him to the vet. It's 10 P.M. when the vet finally delivers the bad news: the dog has cancer and should be put to sleep. You're so tired, you can't stop crying.

Could it get any worse? Of course it could. At play practice the next day, one of your cast members accidentally trips you. Falling hard on your right wrist, you hear something crack. Not only does it hurt like crazy, but an hour later you're riding home from the doctor with your arm in a cast. It's broken. If you get to perform in the play, you'll have to wear the cast.

Questions to Think On

- *Pretty bad week, huh? Does all of this bad stuff happening to you mean God doesn't care about you anymore?*
- *Why would God allow all of these things to occur?*
- *When bad things do happen to you or your family, do you sometimes think God has taken a vacation or do you just take it as it comes?*
- *Mom and Dad: Talk about why bad things happen to even those who call God their Father.*

What Does God Have to Say?

Are not five sparrows sold for two pennies? Yet not one of them is forgotten by God. Indeed, the very hairs of your head are all numbered. Don't be afraid; you are worth more than many sparrows. Luke 12:6–7

How precious to me are your thoughts, O God! How vast is the sum of them! Were I to count them, they would outnumber the grains of sand. When I awake, I am still with you. Psalm 139:17–18

88 ■ Promises, Promises

What If...

Dad, it's the end of summer and you've been working hard for a long time. In fact, because of some family emergencies this year and last, you used up all your vacation days traveling to other cities to spend time with sick relatives.

But you haven't complained. Even the sixty-hour weeks in the middle of that July heat wave didn't wear you down. Most Saturdays you've had to work, though your Sundays off have been a great time to reconnect with our family.

It's now one week before school starts and we're all anxious to do something this Saturday. Mom suggests going for a hike. While you would like something a little less active you promise you'll do whatever we want to do.

On Wednesday night the phone rings. Answering it, you find out it's Pete. He says he and a few other guys from Sunday school are going fishing at a small mountain lake rumored to have six-pound trout in it.

"Sounds great," you say. "When?"

"This Saturday."

"Fishing? With the guys? This Saturday?" you say. "I'd love... "

Just then you remember you promised us you'd go hiking this weekend.

But I've been working hard, you think. *I deserve a little time to do what I want to do. I haven't had any of that time in months.*

It's obvious you've got a minor dilemma on your hands. Do you go fishing because you know you deserve it, or do you spend time with us because you know we deserve it?

Questions to Think On

• *What would you do?*

- *Is it easy for you to keep your word, or do you sometimes want to change plans?*
- *Have you ever broken your word before? When?*
- *Dads have a lot of pressure to try to be the perfect leaders. Are you comfortable with knowing that only God is perfect or do you want to be perfect, too?*

What Does God Have to Say?

Simply let your "Yes" be "Yes," and your "No," "No"; anything beyond this comes from the evil one.   **Matthew 5:37**

So I strive always to keep my conscience clear before God and man.   **Acts 24:16**

89 ■ Unhappy Camper

What If...

Your softball team is on a losing streak. You tell yourself it's not like it's life or death or anything. But losing all the time and not getting to play the position you think you should... well, it's hard to take sometimes.

The coach is a hothead, too–not only at the games, but also at practices. He has high expectations, and since your team can't seem to win a game, his blood boils even more. No, he doesn't swear, he's just a screamer.

One day, you and a few teammates are sitting on the third base bench looking out into the field before practice, waiting for the coach to get there with the equipment. That's when you start.

"Do you guys ever feel like quitting?" you ask them.

One player says yes, but the others say nothing.

"Aren't you sick of losing? Sick of being yelled at? Aren't you tired of seeing the same people pitching all the time and never getting anyone out? I know coaches always have their favorites, but when their main players can't get the ball over the plate, don't you think they should make a few changes?"

One of the others says something about not being able to play shortstop, and being able to throw players out much better than the shortstop you have.

That sets you off even more. You immediately start in on the whole team, position by position. After listening a couple more minutes to your complaining, one of your friends gives you this look that says *shut up*. You turn around... there's your coach standing right behind you.

"Oh, hi, Coach," your friend says. "How long you been standing there?"

"Long enough."

After practice he calls you over to talk. (As in *he talks*, you listen.) He's not happy with your attitude and challenges you to either be a team player or take a hike.

Questions to Think On

- *Would you ever really complain that much?*

- *What do you complain about the most? (Parents can help on this one.)*

- *Complaining and grumbling often mean you're dissatisfied with the way things are. What are ways to express dissatisfaction without complaining?*

- *Mom and Dad: How can complaining short-circuit the feeling of contentment God wants you to have in whatever circumstances he's placed you?*

What Does God Have to Say?

Don't grumble against each other, brothers, or you will be judged. The Judge is standing at the door!   **James 5:9**

"Stop grumbling among yourselves," Jesus answered.
                                                    John 6:43

90 ■ Early riser

What If...

Waking up and getting ready for school has always been tough. It's not that you stay up late, it's just that you're not a morning person. When the alarm goes off at 7:15 you sleep right through it. Then when Mom comes in at 7:20, you wish you could continue sleeping–but you know you can't.

"Breakfast is in ten minutes," she always says. "If you want it hot, you better get dressed and come on out."

So you lumber out of bed, sleepwalk through putting your clothes on and do a dazed shuffle into the kitchen for some food.

For some reason, however, this morning you wake up at 6:55–and can't go back to sleep. You dress and walk out to the kitchen, surprising Mom.

"What's for breakfast?" you say, almost in a chipper tone.

"What are you doing up so early?" she asks.

"Couldn't sleep, so I thought I'd just face the world a little earlier. You don't have to make anything today, I'll just have cereal."

"Sounds fine to me."

Now it's 7:30 and you're already dressed and fed. With

no homework to catch up on, all you have to do is make your bed and brush your teeth. School doesn't start for an hour... what are you going to do now?

You could read that new book you bought at the book fair. You could go watch a tape or some cartoons. Or... there's your Bible next to your bed that you never seem to have time for.

Questions to Think On

- *Be honest: what would you do?*
- *How motivated are you to read your Bible at all?*
- *What would it take to help motivate and discipline you to open it up a few times a week?*
- *Mom and Dad: Talk about your own Bible reading and prayer habits, good and bad.*

What Does God Have to Say?

But Jesus often withdrew to lonely places and prayed.

Luke 5:16

If you remain in me and my words remain in you, ask whatever you wish, and it will be given you.   **John 15:7**

91 ■ Follow the Leader?

What If...

One of the best parts about being in grade school is the chance to spend the night with friends. You get a measure of freedom, can eat all night, watch movies... and be crazy (with limits, of course).

One Friday night, you're at a birthday sleep–over. It's just like always: pizza, presents, cake, games, videos, soda. Yep, you're having a blast.

About midnight, the parents of the house say it's time to start calming down. They say you can talk and leave the TV on, but no more loud noises. They want to go to bed, so if there's any yelling or screaming, they'll bring the hammer down.

Well, that calms everyone down right away. But lying around in sleeping bags gets everyone going again.

"Ssshhhh, you want to get us in trouble?" someone says.

"Hey, I've got an idea," says the birthday kid. "Let's be real quiet and sneak out the sliding glass door in the back. While you're outside, I'll grab some eggs and toilet paper, and we'll go have some fun."

Everyone starts putting on their shoes and heading toward the door. Even though you know the kid's parents (and yours) would flip if they knew you were out that late doing this stuff, no one says anything about whether or not this is such a great idea.

Questions to Think On

- *It sounds like you're stuck. You either go... or stay there by yourself (which wouldn't look too good). What is something you could say to keep everyone from getting into trouble?*

- *If you were able to bring everyone back to reality, what would that protect them from in the future?*

- *How do you react when the crowd wants to do one thing that isn't a good idea, and you know the right thing to do?*

- *Mom and Dad: What will the consequences be when you find out that your child snuck out at this sleep-over and egged and TP'd houses?*

What Does God Have to Say?

My son, if sinners entice you, do not give in to them.

Proverbs 1:10

A violent man entices his neighbor and leads him down a path that is not good.

Proverbs 16:29

92 ■ To Go for the Goal, You've Got to Pay the Toll

What If...

Your older brother is a good basketball player. You've been playing against him for a while to improve your game, but he's naturally *way* ahead of your ability. You know you should play more, but you're the type who gets bored easily. Unless someone's shooting with you, you usually don't bother practicing.

After the season ends, your coach tells you that, in order to play more, you are going to have to start practicing. For a couple of weeks after the season, that's what you do. Every night, you go outside and shoot right-handed lay-

ups, side shots, free throws, long shots—you even start dribbling the ball between your legs. But you soon get tired
and start to find other things to do inside the house.

Now that it's summer, one of your friends invites you to
the basketball camp he usually attends, and you beg us to
pay the $75 to let you go. It is a stretch for us, but we come
up with the cash. The week is great. Not only do you learn
a lot about the sport, you also get to play tons of games
against teams made up of guys your own age. It is an
intense week, but well worth it. Plus, the coach comments
to you that you have a good shot and show real potential.

Again, for the first few weeks after the camp, you are out
shooting every day. But then those distractions come: TV,
going over to your friend's house to play Super Nintendo
and listening to CDs.

To be honest, you can see from your year on the team—
and the week at camp—that basketball requires more dedication and energy than you are willing to give. Even
though you are good at basketball (and even like it), you
enjoy watching TV and playing games more than practicing a sport.

Questions to Think On

- *Are you the type who can be dedicated to a few things, or are you a little lazier? Why do you think that is?*
- *Why is it so tempting to be lazy?*
- *What do you think are the consequences of being lazy?*
- *What do you think are the rewards of dedication and work?*

What Does God Have to Say?

Lazy hands make a man poor, but diligent hands bring
wealth. **Proverbs 10:4**

I went past the field of the sluggard, past the vineyard of the man who lacks judgment; thorns had come up everywhere, the ground was covered with weeds, and the stone wall was in ruins. I applied my heart to what I observed and learned a lesson from what I saw: A little sleep, a little slumber, a little folding of the hands to rest–and poverty will come on you like a bandit and scarcity like an armed man.   **Proverbs 24:30–34**

93 ■ Charting His Own Course (Sort Of)

What If...

One of us kids is a handful. Since you're such a great parent, the kid isn't bad or anything, just... preoccupied. His mind is always on a different planet.

Whenever it's time to clean his room, he goes in and finds other things to do instead. It doesn't matter what–pencil games, reading a book, building forts or just looking around at his posters. It usually takes three or four rounds of threats and reminders to get him at least to get his stuff off of the floor.

At Christmas and on birthdays it takes you even more reminders to get him to write thank-you notes. And when it comes to helping out around the house and doing his chores... he's nearly impossible.

Again, this child isn't a bad kid; he just has his mind on other things besides what he is supposed to do. At times he *is* a little lazy, but... he is also very affectionate. He loads you up with hugs and kisses and "I love you's."

Even with all of the joy he brings to the household, your patience is wearing thin. You have tried many, many things to get him to clue into the responsibilities he needs to take more seriously. You have withheld his allowance, cut back on TV time, not let him invite his friends over on weekends. But even these tactics don't work all that well–at least for very long.

Questions to Think On

- *How patient would you be with a child like this?*
- *How are we kids different, and how do you treat us differently because of it?*
- *What does God teach you through us (especially in this area of patience)?*
- *Is there anything we need to do to try to make it a bit easier for you as a parent?*

What Does God Have to Say?

And we pray this in order that you may live a life worthy of the Lord and may please him in every way: bearing fruit in every good work, growing in the knowledge of God, being strengthened with all power according to his glorious might so that you may have great endurance and patience.

Colossians 1:10–11

You too, be patient and stand firm, because the Lord's coming is near.   James 5:8

94 ■ The Unpardonable Sin?

What If...

Our family is a week or so away from going on a campout together and you are really looking forward to it.

Dad borrows a propane stove, some cots and other gear, but he does something really cool: he buys this huge six-person tent! When he brings it home and takes it out of the box, he suggests we all try to put it up in the side yard. After it is up, it looks great. Then Dad says that maybe a few of us should test it out–tonight!

After a fun night out in the tent, everyone knows that this year's camping trip is going to be the best. Dad leaves the tent up to air out for a few days before it is packed up and put with the other camping gear.

One night, while everyone sleeps, the unthinkable happens: someone steals the tent. We get up in the morning and it is gone! And we are leaving for our camping trip the next day. Talk about major disappointment... and major anger. Everyone is pretty hacked off that someone would actually steal a tent right out of someone's yard.

Dad works all day trying to round up another tent from some of his buddies. Finally, he finds three two-person pup tents that will hold the whole family.

Well, it turns out to be a fun trip, but everyone is still mad that we can't use the nice, big tent–especially you!

Two weeks later there's a knock on our door. As Dad opens it, you and Mom are standing next to him. It's a teenager and his dad. The teenager starts talking and admits that he took our tent... and sold it. He can't pay us back yet, but will as soon as he can earn the money. The guy's dad apologizes and says he'll make sure his son follows through.

Questions to Think On

- *What would you be thinking about the teenage kid if this happened to you?*
- *How easy would it be for you to forgive him?*
- *How easy is it for you to forget about another's wrongdoing after he or she apologizes?*
- *Mom and Dad: Why is forgiveness so important? What can unforgiveness do to you?*

What Does God Have to Say?

Then Peter came to Jesus and asked, "Lord, how many times shall I forgive my brother when he sins against me? Up to seven times?"

Jesus answered, "I tell you, not seven times, but seventy-seven times."   Matthew 18:21–22

Be kind and compassionate to one another, forgiving each other, just as in Christ God forgave you.   Ephesians 4:32

95 ■ The Confused Sub

What If...

It's Monday morning and you're heading to your classroom–as usual. As you get closer, you see a couple of your friends, so you run to find out what they did over the weekend.

Walking into class, you notice that things aren't quite right. The sentence on the blackboard that you usually have to correct isn't there. There's also no coffee smell. Looking over in the corner you see an older woman sitting at the desk where your teacher usually sits.

One of your friends starts to get this look in her eye.

"What are you thinking?" you say.

"It looks like we have a substitute today, doesn't it?" Nicole says.

"So?"

"So, why don't we have some fun?"

"Whaddaya mean?"

"Let's grab a couple other girls and get them in on this."

"On what?" you demand.

"Megan, Susan, you want to play an innocent little trick on the substitute?" she whispers as the other two girls approach.

"Sure," they agree, giggling.

"OK, I'll be Megan. Megan, you be Susan. Susan, you be Sharon. And Sharon, you be me. We'll sit in each other's seats and see how long we can go before she finds out. I bet we can fool her all day."

"Sounds great," Megan says. "But we should tell the kids around us so they don't give it away."

"Good idea, Megan," Nicole says.

"OK, we better get in our seats."

When the teacher calls roll, everyone plays her part perfectly. The teacher doesn't suspect a thing.

Though you thought it was mean to fool this substitute, you went along with it because it did seem fairly innocent.

Questions to Think On

• *What should you really have done?*

• *When playing a trick on others—including adults—can't really hurt them, does that make it OK to fool them?*

• *What would the consequences have been from the principal if he had caught you? How about at home?*

- *If your friends at school really tried something like this to fool a teacher, what would you say if you felt it was unkind to do?*

What Does God Have to Say?

Love is patient, love is kind. It does not envy, it does not boast, it is not proud. It is not rude, it is not self-seeking, it is not easily angered, it keeps no record of wrongs.

·1 Corinthians 13:4–5

For rulers hold no terror for those who do right, but for those who do wrong. Do you want to be free from fear of the one in authority? Then do what is right and he will commend you. Romans 13:3

96 ■ Look Out for the Power of Evil!

What If...

You've lived next door to Amy ever since you can remember. You went through kindergarten and most of grade school together.

But in fourth grade, Amy's parents got a divorce. Her dad moved out one day and now Amy only sees him about once a month. Amy's mom tried hard to keep family life normal, including going back to work to keep the house. Unfortunately, Amy's dad wasn't too consistent with his child support payments, so they eventually had to sell their home and move to an apartment.

Amy still goes to the same school as you, so you see her every day, but you notice she's changed. She brings these books about magic and the supernatural to school all the time and reads them at recess and lunch. She doesn't play anymore; she mainly keeps to herself. When she does talk, it's always about the latest book she's read or another scary movie she's seen at her dad's house while watching HBO.

To try to see what's going on, you invite her to your birthday sleep-over with a few other girls. When she gets there, she's got this big backpack and a sleeping bag.

"Have I got a game for us later after your parents go to bed," she says.

Amy seems agitated the whole time she's at your house; she even reads while the rest of the girls and you go play sardines. About 11 P.M., after Mom and Dad go to bed (with instructions that lights out will be 1 A.M.–if everything stays quiet), she pulls out this thing called an Ouija Board. She starts explaining how it works, turns out the lights and turns on a flashlight.

Before she can get started, Dad comes down. When he sees what's going on, he puts the board back in the box and says Amy can take it with her in the morning. Then he says, "Lights out."

Questions to Think On

- *Amy has filled her mind with some pretty bad stuff since her dad left. Who do you think she is being influenced by?*

- *When you're in grade school, you rarely see Satan working behind the scenes to ruin someone's life. As you get older, it becomes more obvious. What do you know about Satan?*

- *Though it's not good to dwell on him, it is a good idea to know how he works. Mom and Dad, explain how his influence starts in the mind and then works its way to behavior.*

- *Mom and Dad: What else do you know about Satan's plans for humans, God's unique creation?*

What Does God Have to Say?

Be self-controlled and alert. Your enemy the devil prowls around like a roaring lion looking for someone to devour.

1 Peter 5:8

The Lord will rescue me from every evil attack and will bring me safely to his heavenly kingdom.

2 Timothy 4:18

97 ■ What's Worthless?

What If...

It's Saturday night and Mom and Dad are out on a date. That's right, we've hired a sitter and left you and your little sister home. We don't do this very often, but when we do, we always seem to look forward to it.

The sitter says she wants to take your little sister across the street to the playground for a while and asks if you want to come.

"No, there's a TV show on I'd like to watch. I'll be OK by myself. Mom's left me home for an hour at a time. If you're just across the street, I'll be OK. I'll even let the phone ring until the machine picks it up."

"OK, that sounds fine," the sitter replies. "We'll probably be an hour or so."

After they're gone, you grab the TV remote and park yourself on the couch. It's not often you just get to lie around and watch whatever you want.

Instead of checking the *TV Guide*, you just start at channel two and work your way up. There are a few things on that look good, but you want to go through all forty-five channels before you decide on a show. When you get to the top you keep going. Normally, that's when the picture looks all scrambled because those channels are pay-TV. But when you get to channel forty-six, the picture is clean.

Hmmmm, you think. *What's this?*

As the movie continues to play, you recognize it as one of those R-rated movies a few friends from school were talking about a long time ago. It's got a lot of swearing in it, but it also has a lot of comedy. Checking the *TV Guide* again, you read that Cinemax is having a free weekend to try to sign up subscribers. Your attention goes back to the TV where you see a man and a woman kissing in a bathtub.

Questions to Think On

- *You're faced with a choice at this point to change the channel or keep watching. What would you do and why?*
- *We can't monitor everything you look at your whole life. Eventually, you're going to be making all of your own decisions. How are you going to know what's good and what isn't?*
- *Have you talked about the viewing guidelines with Mom and Dad? If not, do so now.*
- *Mom and Dad: Explain why it's so important not to pump a lot of violent or sexual stuff into your brain.*

What Does God Have to Say?

I will set before my eyes no vile thing. The deeds of faithless men I hate; they will not cling to me. Men of perverse heart shall be far from me; I will have nothing to do with evil. **Psalm 101:3–4**

Anyone who lives on milk, being still an infant is not acquainted with the teaching about righteousness. But solid food is for the mature, who by constant use have trained themselves to distinguish good from evil.

Hebrews 5:13-14

Teach me knowledge and good judgment, for I believe in your commands.   **Psalm 119:66**

98 ■ The Costly Deception

What If...

As a father you've always been motivated to provide for your family. You work hard and have given us a good measure of security. No, not everything can be planned for—life on earth doesn't hold many guarantees—but you do your best.

That's why when you notice a newspaper ad talking about an insurance plan that is also a college savings plan, you check it out. You call up the company to get more facts and then make an appointment to meet with one of the agents.

Over a cup of coffee at Denny's one morning, the agent explains the plan. He says that if you start with five thousand dollars, the interest rate will be nearly double what you now make at the bank. "The investments we've selected give a higher return when more is invested," the agent says.

You ask more questions and tell the guy you'll think about it. After discussing it with Mom, you agree that it sounds good. Calling the agent back up, you let him know your decision. He says you've made the right choice.

The following Monday, you fill out a bunch of paperwork and give the agent a check. He explains you'll be getting monthly statements that chart the progress of your account. You feel good that you're providing more life insurance in case something happens to you, while saving for our college educations.

A month goes by and you notice no statements have come in the mail. So you call the agent up. The operator says the line has been disconnected. Suddenly, you get a sick feeling in the pit of your stomach. You realize you've been ripped off by a con artist.

Calling the police you find out you weren't the only one. Dozens of people fell for it. The guy was good.

It takes two months, but they catch the man who scammed you out of your money. It seems he spent it all in a foreign country before coming back to try his scheme again. The cash is gone, but at least he's behind bars. A while later, you see him in court as you're giving your testimony.

Questions to Think On

- *What the guy did was very bad. How would you feel about him in your heart?*
- *Could you ever forgive the man for what he did?*
- *What lessons would you learn from this bad situation?*
- *If you had the chance to talk to him for ten minutes alone, what would you say?*

What Does God Have to Say?

Hatred stirs up dissension, but love covers over all wrongs.
Proverbs 10:12

Forgive us our debts, as we also have forgiven our debtors.
Matthew 6:12

99 ■ What Are You Known For?

What If...

One thing you've noticed is all girls are different. Not just in looks, but also in what they think. Some of your girlfriends are still having a good time playing with their Barbies, while others are talking about the guys they want to "go with." A few *are* "going with" guys and brag about the guys they've kissed! Like Brenda.

Brenda is one of your friends. She's a nice girl, but even the teachers talk about her reputation as a guy chaser. Mom and Dad have seen her in action, too. At the school skating party a few weeks ago, we noticed her with one of the guys near the arcade. She was hanging all over him and trying to kiss him like they were teenagers or something. The guy was attempting to fight her off and finish his game, but we could tell he wasn't trying too hard. Mom talked to you about her later, mentioning something about Brenda not having a dad at home, and that's probably one reason why she acts that way.

The other girls talk about Brenda—a lot. Some, you can tell, are jealous, while others (like you) think she's really making a fool of herself.

One evening, Brenda calls and tells you her mom is letting her have a party on Saturday, a coed party with music and dancing. She not only wants you to come, but also asks if you'll help decorate.

"A coed party at Brenda's?" Mom says after you ask her if you can go. "I'm not sure that's a great idea. Is her mom going to be home?"

"Yes, Mom," you reply. "But I doubt she'll be downstairs watching everything. That wouldn't be cool."

"Let me think about it and talk to your father," she says.

Questions to Think On

- *Would you want her to say OK, or are you thinking this may not be the best party to go to?*
- *Do you know anyone at school with this type of reputation?*
- *What do you think your reputation is? What do you want it to be?*
- *Mom and Dad: Would you allow your child to go to this party? When making decisions about what your kids can do for fun in the future, how important to you are the reputations of those they will be with?*

What Does God Have to Say?

A good name is more desirable than great riches; to be esteemed is better than silver or gold.   **Proverbs 22:1**

100 ■ No Comment for Everything

What If...

"Your dad and I are going shopping for a few hours," Mom tells you. "You and your big sister have a good afternoon. Oh, and don't forget to do your chores."

A few hours with just my sis and me on a beautiful Saturday afternoon, you think. *Hmmm, what can we do?*

"I'm going into the family room to watch TV," your sister announces.

"TV? On a day like this? What a waste of time!"

"Sorry, I didn't sleep too well last night, so I'm just looking for a nice couch to take a nap on. Try to be quiet, OK?"

"OK."

Heading into your room, you notice it needs a little straightening up. Forty-five minutes later the room is immaculate. You even cleaned your closet and under the bed! *Mom and Dad will really be impressed with this,* you think.

Looking out your window you notice that leaves have covered the ground. *Dad always has to rake those leaves alone. Maybe I'll...*

And with that you head outside, grab a rake from the garage and start raking. Taking only one short soda break, you finish the job in just about an hour. You even put all the leaves in plastic bags and stack them neatly on the sidewalk for the trash man to pick up on Monday. The yard looks great!

Going back inside, you notice that the kitchen is a mess. *Might as well go for it.* And in just twenty minutes all the dishes are washed and the counters cleaned. *All this work will probably double my allowance this week,* you think, while also wondering how you're going to spend the extra cash.

Over the next hour and a half you keep up the pace: vacuuming the whole house, folding clothes, dusting, straightening up. Just as you're about ready to go sweep the garage, Mom and Dad drive up.

Getting out of the car, we head in with our packages. No comments about the yard. As you follow us around, asking how our shopping was, we walk back to our bedroom—through the kitchen, the living room and past your bedroom. Not a word comes from our lips about the shape of the house.

By the time you're in bed you realize we didn't notice. You got no rewards, no thanks, no nothing.

Questions to Think On

- *How would you feel if you did all that stuff and didn't get rewarded, not even with a thank-you?*
- *Do you ever think God feels the way you do? (That is, is he doing*

stuff for you all the time that you're not thanking him for?)

- *Would you consider yourself a thankful person? Do you find it easy or hard to recognize when something's been done for you?*
- *What would it take for you to be more thankful?*

What Does God Have to Say?

I have not stopped giving thanks for you, remembering you in my prayers.   Ephesians 1:16

Give thanks in all circumstances, for this is God's will for you in Christ Jesus.   1 Thessalonians 5:18

101 ■ Inside Choices

What If...

There are a lot of things that make you happy. Some of these last for a short while, others for a longer period of time. In all honesty, say which things would make you the most happy:

- Getting a new bike or taking a trip to the beach with the family for a whole week.
- Becoming best friends with the most popular person in your grade or having a not-so-popular neighbor kid become a Christian at your church one day.
- Taking a trip at Christmas to be with grandparents or staying home and getting more presents.
- Going to a water slide park for the day or spending the day helping Mom clean the house of a widow who is too old to clean it herself.

- Breaking your arm *or* getting a new Super Nintendo game.
- Going out to lunch after church *or* handing out food baskets to poor people in the park.
- Learning you have a treatable cancer condition *or* going through all of your school years as a normal kid with no problems.

Questions to Think On

- *Some of these choices aren't that tough, are they? One thing I've learned as a parent is that what we place value on determines our happiness more than the absence of trouble. How do you think "bad" circumstances can help us be happy?*
- *Does getting new stuff really make us happy?*
- *This is a tough one: What do you think is the difference between happiness and joy? Which would you rather have?*
- *Mom and Dad: Why is it so tempting to go after short-term happiness instead of longer-term joy?*

What Does God Have to Say?

I tell you that in the same way there is more rejoicing in heaven over one sinner who repents than over ninety-nine righteous persons who do not need to repent.

Luke 15:7

Consider it pure joy, my brothers, whenever you face trials of many kinds, because you know that the testing of your faith develops perseverance. Perseverance must finish its work so that you may be mature and complete, not lacking anything.

James 1:2-4

Looking for a devotional your teen will read?

If the Pasta Wiggles, Don't Eat It!
(And Other Good Advice)
Wise Words to Tickle Your Funnybone and Make You Think!

New! from Martha Bolton

From the man whose tombstone merely reads, "Been here. Had a good time. Gone." to the diving lesson offered at a local pool by a non-swimmer frightened of the water, award-winning humorist Martha Bolton's uproarious teen devotional is sure to bring a smile to young mouths as well as godly encouragement to their searching hearts.

This book offers light-hearted-but-serious inspiration for growing closer to God and imitating His ways. It is packed with 90 hilarious devotions designed to entertain and instruct young people in practical spiritual living. Best of all, promises Martha, "the Devotional Police aren't going to come to your house and cite you if you exceed the page limit." **$8.99**